A Heart-Pounding Guide to Passionate Sex

Dr. Stephanie Buehler

Psychologist & Sex Therapist

Director, The Buehler Institute

Dedicated to my beloved Mark, for being my best friend, husband, co-parent, and lover, and to passionate, loving couples everywhere.

Table of Contents

How to Use this Book

You could skip the first section of this book and get straight to what everybody thinks is the secret of good sex--the techniques and toys that lead to better arousal and orgasm.

But you would miss the point. Good sex happens as much between your ears as it does between the sheets, no matter how long you've been together.

I strongly recommend that you read the beginning of the book, even if you think you have a healthy sense of your sexuality. (You may have even bought this E-book because you think it's your partner that has a problem.) As you will learn, sexuality isn't just about sex!

PART ONE: Passionate Sex

Chapter 1

1. Passionate Sex: Every Couple's Desire

Sex and passion. That's what every couple says they're after, but you'd think that passionate sex was something that you win in a lottery drawing. Or that having a great life-long sex partner is based on luck. And many people think that the odds of experiencing passion in a long-term relationship are about as slim.

The fact is that you can create passionate sex in your marriage or long-term partnership. Even if your sex life has dwindled to the most miserly trickle, you can revive your sex life--if you want to. And it doesn't cost anything or require rocket science to make it happen.

What it does require is time, a loving attitude, and a willingness to experiment.

But before we get down to the nitty gritty--the lovemaking techniques that every couple needs to know that I write about in the second part of this book--let's look at some reasons that passionate sex disappears like a puddle of water on a hot day, and then some ways to start quenching your sexual needs.

After all, to get to where you want to go, you have to know how you got where you are.

How Do You Know If Sex Is Passionate?

How is passion defined? As a sex therapist, this is a question I frequently ask my clients. Let's see how people typically define this elusive emotion.

Greg: *Passion means that my partner shows me that she wants me, really wants me. She expresses her love, and she doesn't act like sex is a chore or a bother.*

Amy: *When my partner is more aggressive and really gets into it, that's what I call passionate sex.*

Joe: *To me, passionate sex happens when we really take our time to please each other.*

Kathy: *I think my husband and I have the most passionate sex after we've just finished up an intensely close conversation over a glass of wine. For us, there has to be a connection outside the bedroom to be passionate in the bedroom.*

Who's right? They all are, of course! Passionate sex can be described as Masters and Johnson famously said, "More than body parts and friction." Passionate sex . . .

Makes your senses feel fully aware and alive;

Eases your worries and gives you a moment of peace;

Makes you feel more connected;

Drains away doubts about love;

Soothes and replenishes your body;

And last, but not least, feels fantastic!

It's possible, though, that you are reading this book because you have NEVER experienced passionate sex. Or you have, but you've long ago forgot how the steps to the dance. You may be wondering what sex is all about, or trying to figure out why having passionate sex is important.

Don't worry. Whatever the state of your sex life, keep reading, and you'll have lots of ways to kindle, or rekindle, the sexual spark in your relationship.

When Lack of Passion Becomes a Problem

So what's up with wanting to have passionate sex, anyway? Part of it probably has to do with the way the media portrays sex. You see people taking off their clothes and getting right into it. Except for the short-lived cable TV program, "Tell Me You Love Me," we really don't have a realistic portrayal of the struggles real couples have around sex. And we certainly aren't taught how to resolve them.

Early on in your relationship, your heart, mind, and soul are on fire. For many couples, that quick, hot connection blots out any awkwardness, embarrassment, shame, or guilt you may have about sex.

Then, too, when you are dating, you can better hide your sexual struggles. After a night of lovemaking, you can go home and regroup. You can control when the next sexual encounter is going to happen; there's no one already waiting for you to come to bed at night. Since you do not live with your partner, you don't have to deal with your sexuality all that frequently, so you can avoid problems.

Once you are spending most of your time together, living under the same roof, there might not be anywhere to hide the fact that:

- You really aren't as interested in sex as you initially let your partner believe

- You aren't that excited about the way your partner makes love now that the initial heat has cooled

- You don't feel all that great about yourself as a lover, either, come to think of it

- You know things could be better, but you have no idea where to begin.

Now you're stuck. Maybe you go to bed night after night wondering how to make things change. Because almost anything is better than talking openly about sex. It's just too embarrassing. Too intimate. Too...open. Right? Wrong.

The problem is that you don't know *how* to talk about sex. But no worries, that's what you're going to read about next.

Chapter 2

2. Sex Talk

Why does talking about sex make grown men and women zip their mouths closed? For many reasons. One is that most people learn how to talk about sex on the schoolyard. Schoolyard talk reflects what adults convey to children about sex, that sex is "dirty" and "naughty." As an adult, your commonsense thought is that you're not supposed to, and probably don't want to, talk about sex that way with someone you love.

So then you end up not talking at all.

Another is shame. Talking about sex as an adult to another adult means admitting that sex is important to you, and you were probably brought up to ignore its importance. You don't want to tell your partner what you want, because that would mean that you like sex, and that might be shameful, as well as embarrassing.

Then there's the other belief that if your partner knew you well, he or she would simply know what turns you on. That's a lovely fantasy, but the only person who understood that was your mom when you were an infant, and you wanted only a few things: food, a diaper, a cuddle, or a nap. There is no way your partner can guess everything about your sexual likes and dislikes.

So now you're back to having to overcome your embarrassment in order to talk about sex.

But the sad fact is that if you're not talking, you're still communicating. And unfortunately, what your partner thinks you are communicating is that you don't think your relationship is important or worth the effort. After a year or two--or a decade--of this, is it any wonder that so many couples end up with bad feelings and a loss of passion?

If you think about it, in a way, much of what sex is all about is communication. Somehow, you invite one another to show up for a session of touching and, most likely, intercourse and orgasm. But instead of "talking" about something exciting like how tingly you feel, you're "talking" about something that compares to the weather or what you ate for breakfast! How boring is that?

So if you want to have good sex, you have to learn how to talk, both verbally and nonverbally.

You have to learn how to communicate verbally, because you have to tell your partner what you like and don't like, what turns you on and what turns you off.

And you have to communicate nonverbally, through the way you express yourself physically to one another.

Granted, even couples that are good "conversationalists" about sex do run out of things to "talk" about. So you have to find a way to keep the dialogue going.

Boring, routine sex isn't the way to do it. In fact, you run the risk of ruining the whole relationship by slacking off in the bedroom. Listen to a complaint that you might hear in the office of a sex therapist:

Jane: *Every time we have sex, it's the same thing. He touches my breasts, then 'down there.' Then he's on top of me, and we're done in a minute. There's no kissing any more, and he falls asleep about 5 minutes after he finishes. Is it any surprise that I don't want to have sex all that much? The thing is, my lack of interest could kill our marriage, so I have to do something about it. But how am I supposed to tell him that he's just not very good in bed?*

Carlos: *Maria and I have sex every Saturday night, at the same time, in the same way. She says I should be grateful that she "lets" me have sex. It isn't very satisfying, she doesn't want to hug or kiss or even let me touch her all that much. I love her, but sometimes I think I'd be better off making love to one of those "sex dolls"!*

Does either Jane or Carlos sound like they're having much fun? Do you think their partners are really enjoying themselves, either? It all sounds so . . . dull! And sad! So much hurt and pain could be avoided if they told their partner what pleased them, and asked their partner to do the same in turn.

Starting the Sex Conversation

So how do you talk about sex? Well, one place to start is to give yourself permission to treat sex as a topic of conversation like any other. Whether you think sex is a splendid form of entertainment, a sacred act of love, or an obligation to your marriage or your partner, you have thoughts and opinions about sex. You also have values, beliefs, and experiences.

Still not sure how to get things rolling? Embarrassed? Feel weird? That's okay. Here are some ice breakers and conversation starters that can get you and your partner conversing about sex:

- When did you first realize that you were a boy / a girl? What did you think about your own sex? What did you think about the opposite sex?

- Do you remember how old you were when you started to feel sexual urges? What was that like for you?

- What sorts of love or sex scenes in movies or books really turn you on?

- What did you learn about sex from your parents? From church or temple? From school?

- What is the silliest thing you ever heard about sex? How did you find out the truth?

- Do you have a bad experience that you feel safe enough to talk about?

- What is the one thing that you want from our sex life that you're not getting? Why haven't you asked?

- What is the most embarrassing thing about sex? Why are you embarrassed about it? What would make it less embarrassing?

- Why do you want to make love to me? Why do you want me to make love to you?

- What part of sex is the most (fun, exciting, loving, passionate, warm, boring) for you?

- If we could make love anywhere in the world, where would you want it to be? Why?

- What do you need me to do to help you get in the mood?

- How can we make it easier or safer to talk about sex?

- How have your ideas about sex changed now that we've been together for a while?

- Is there something about your sexuality you'd like to tell me that you've not been able to tell me before?

- What is your favorite time of day to have sex? Why?

- How do you feel when I don't want to make love with you? How should I let you know that I don't want to make love without hurting your feelings?

- What is the most erotic thing you've ever seen? Ever done?

- What song or type of music makes you feel aroused?

What if your partner is too embarrassed to participate with you? Then start with there, asking your partner if he or she is willing to talk to you about why they are embarrassed.

What if you're too embarrassed to start? An alternative to talking, of course, is writing answers to one another in a private journal that perhaps gets left in a special, safe place. You could then let one another know when you have written something that you want your partner to read.

Eventually, you may come to feel more comfortable expressing your sexual thoughts, perhaps enough to have more open verbal discussions over time.

How Sexual Communication Changes

Your sexual vocabulary also grows with experience. If the two of you have been in a rut, doing the same things over and over again, then there isn't much to talk about. That's why it's important to have a good sexual repertoire, or knowledge, about all the basic but different ways of pleasing your partner and exploring your sexuality, both alone and together.

Just having a combination of good communication and good lovemaking technique can really improve your sex life. Taking the time and effort to invest in a good sex life shows real love, caring, and intimacy for your partner. And that's a big part of how you can keep passion alive in your relationship.

Giving Feedback for Passionate Sex

As you read this book and start to learn your partner's body, you might also be surprised to find that you learn more about your own sexual wants and needs.

It may be that you never realized you needed or desired a lighter or firmer touch. If you are a woman, you may realize that you only like your genitals to be gently stroked; if you're a man, perhaps that you like your testicles caressed during oral sex.

There is no right or wrong way to make love; it is all a matter of preferences. So giving your partner feedback about you like or don't like is part of increasing passion and pleasure. That's why it's important that you both learn how to give—and receive—feedback from your lover.

Here are a few guidelines that I offer to the couples that I see:

Keep feedback to a minimum while you are in the early stages of exploring one another's bodies. You don't want to make your partner overly self-conscious or anxious during lovemaking.

Later, you can give feedback nonverbally during lovemaking by making various sounds, like moaning or sighing when something feels particularly good.

The time to give more detailed feedback is after lovemaking, by light of day, in your clothing. That's because people feel very vulnerable about being given feedback about their lovemaking technique.

Use what my colleague Patti Britton, Ph.D. calls a "feedback sandwich." Tell your partner something that you liked, then ask for something you'd like them to do for you, then compliment him or her again.

So, for example, you might say, "I love the way you kissed my neck. When we make love next time, could you go a little easier when you caress my breasts? A light touch would feel as good as those kisses. And the way you licked my ear really sent me over the edge!"

Don't take feedback personally. Remember, this is about learning a technique that best fits your partner's needs, not about your ego and the need to feel like a naturally gifted lover. Do what you can to make it safe for your partner to tell you what they need.

Do your best to remember the feedback that your partner gave you. If you don't remember, ask to be gently reminded or shown. Showing that you listened is part of passionate lovemaking.

Chapter 3

3. Having Sex, or Making Love?

It's a common complaint among individuals and couples that feel passion has drained out of their relationship, and it goes like this: Once upon a time, as a couple they felt that when they had sex, it really meant something. They felt a true connection and enjoyment in their sex play. Instead of just having sex, they were really making love.

Then it came to pass that one, or both, of them felt that sex became mechanical, that they were going through the motions to "achieve" orgasm. At long last, things became so mechanical that one, or both, or them began to avoid sex altogether. And before long, they found themselves wondering why they had ever gotten married in the first place.

Like the difference between drinking orange soda and orange juice, this typical tale demonstrates the difference between "having sex" and "making love." The first sounds like a job that you clock into so you can survive in your relationship. Or maybe something to be checked off, like brushing your teeth--something you do for hygiene. The other is an activity that you anticipate with excitement, one that couples typically describe as having meaning beyond the physical realm.

People usually know the difference between "having sex" and "making love," but just in case, here's how to tell you're having the former, and not the latter:

- You have the same emotional connection with your partner that you have with a bottle of lotion

- You don't have anything good to watch on TV so you might as well get off

- The foreplay lasts about as long as a commercial

- The orgasm is like getting a good massage, but without having to pay a tip

- The after play consists of one (or both) of you serenading each other with snores

You're making love if...

- You feel that it's just you and your lover, and that nothing else matters

- You feel cherished, content, and complete when you part

- You would rather be here than anywhere else

- The foreplay is long and exciting

- The orgasm makes you feel alive and vital, or relaxed and soothed

- The after play is almost (or sometimes) better than the foreplay

I'm not saying there isn't room for both having sex and making love, even in a long-term relationship. Sometimes an orange pop is just what you need!

But you have to understand which is which. You need to know why you're showing up, and whether your partner is on the same page. If you both agree to have sex for the sake of sex, go for it! But just as orange soda doesn't offer many nutrients, having sex doesn't really feed you, emotionally, physically, or for some people, spiritually.

If you want to make love, that requires a little finesse. A little persuasion. A little technique. Sometimes a little patience, sometimes a lot of love. And it's in the effort, for couples that have been together awhile, that the passion they seek actually occurs.

Most couples don't realize that learning to make love to a partner can take months, even years. The fact is that people usually grow up with inhibitions. They have heard negative messages about sex from home, school, and church. They may have had some negative sexual experiences, too, that make them feel confused about sex. And finally, they may not really know what turns them on, nor communicate it to their partner.

Gina's Story

When I met Brett, I couldn't have been happier. Although there was no way for him to know, I had been date raped in college and had been turned off to relationships ever since.

But Brett made it easy to fall in love. He respected me, and like me, he wanted to take it slow. We waited until we were engaged before we had intercourse. I remember being a little disappointed to have waited so long, because the sex wasn't all that great, but Brett was so gentle and caring, I didn't have the heart to say anything.

Brett also had what I considered to be kind of a low sex drive. We only seemed to have sex two or three times a month. But since I had had such a bad experience, I didn't want to say anything. And I also did not want to hurt Brett's feelings. So even though I had some concerns, I just put them in the back of my mind. I figured everything would just work itself out. We got married and went to Fiji for the honeymoon. We only had sex once, and it was just so so. Brett insisted on making love that first night and he was so tired he just kind of lost his erection.

When we got home we went back to our usual lovemaking schedule, which is to say hardly ever. I think I would have gone on that way forever, but then something funny happened. My youngest sister got married about a year after us, and she came back from the honeymoon walking on a cloud. At the first opportunity she had, she pulled me aside and said, "You never told me how exciting it would be!"

I faked a chuckle and made some kind of lame joke. But I could feel my throat get choked up. The next time Brett and I made love, I couldn't help myself. I started to cry, and I knew I had to say something.

The funny thing is, Brett admitted he had felt some of the same frustration with our sex life as I had, but hadn't wanted to hurt me. He sometimes felt like I was somewhere else while we had sex, and he was never sure if I liked what he was doing.

So we had agreed to forgive each other and to try starting over again. We got some instructional books on lovemaking technique, and we learned how to tell one another what we liked and didn't like.

Things are much better now. We both look forward to lovemaking sessions, and while we're never going to win a contest for most sex in a week, it is something much more frequent. Moreover, I am much more comfortable with my own sexuality now and can show Brett how I'm enjoying what he's doing to my body. That helps him get turned on, and somehow sex isn't a problem any more.

So what else could be more fun--and educational--than learning how to make love to the most important person in your life? (Okay, it's not quite the education your parents had in mind, but so what!)

When you later turn to the sexual information in Part II, you'll find that much of what you're going to learn together has to do with exploration, with finding out what feels good and what feels even better.

I encourage you to go slow and take your time. When you know, really know, your partner's deepest sexual wants and needs, and share the same, then you'll experience the passion you've been missing.

Barriers to Great Sex

Although there are plenty of psychologists and marital therapists to tell you that there is something wrong in your relationship if the sex isn't working, what I have learned as a sex therapist is that, in private, clients complain about a partner's "lack of technique."

Mechanical sex happens when you think there is just one or a few ways to turn your partner on.

If you're male, you may think you just have to tweak your partner's nipples, rub her between her legs, and hop on.

If you're female, you may think you just need to let your partner squeeze your breasts a little, rub you a little down there, and let your partner hop on.

When you are first getting to know one another as lovers, your excitement about being together may be enough to compensate for lack of technique.

But after a few months, or years, of this skimpy script, you may be...

- Avoiding sex

- Feeling resentful about sex

- Seeking chocolate instead of sex

- Wanting another partner for better sex

Many people assume that when the sex gets dull, it means that they are no longer compatible. In fact, that very fear may keep them from saying anything.

After all, if you dare to draw attention to the mediocre sex that you've been having, your partner might notice, too. Together, you might decide that boring sex means it's time to part.

But that makes no sense. If you still love and care about one another, then the sexual part of your relationship can be improved. It's when you don't care about sex any more--nor any other part of your relationship--that tells you your relationship is either kaput or in bad need of repair.

Lack of technique doesn't necessarily mean lack of caring. Partners can lack technique for a variety of different reasons, including:

- Inexperience

- Inhibitions and embarrassment

- Shame and guilt

- Being overly mechanical, disconnecting sex from love

Notice that the words "lazy," "prudish," "cold," or "selfish" aren't listed. Using words like that to describe another's technique show a sense of blame.

I've found that most people aren't really at fault when it comes to poor technique, but they do have a responsibility to be aware of any problems in their sexuality and its expression. For example, if you are inexperienced as a lover, it doesn't do to just avoid the whole area of sex in your relationship.

Let's look at each of these factors in turn to understand the problems they cause, and some solutions to making things better.

Inexperience. Women are more likely than men to be inexperienced sexually. On average, women have 3 to 5 sexual partners in a lifetime, while men may have 10 to 12. Still, there are also men who come into a long-term relationship with very little sexual skill. Just because you have had sexual partners doesn't necessarily mean that you had good quality sex!

Of course, there are also adults who lack experience having made a choice to follow their religion's teachings to abstain from sex before marriage. Even though an adult may intellectually understand that it is okay to enjoy sex once the wedding ceremony has taken place, it can be quite difficult to flip the switch and become an expressive partner willing to experiment sexually.

When one or both partners are inhibited and inexperienced, sex usually ends up being mechanical, sparse, and unsatisfying. There may be a lack of flow to your sexual activity, so that you seem to be stopping and starting as you adjust yourselves for each part of your lovemaking experience.

If you are the more experienced partner, your partner's lack of experience, and their anxiety about it, may make you so tense that you cannot relax and enjoy yourself. Conversely, if you are not as experienced, you may feel pressure to perform, and find yourself upset or even losing interest.

The solution is to accept your inexperience, but instead of seeing yourself as a clod in bed, view yourself as a student of love and sex. If your partner is more experienced, ask him or her to be your teacher. Sometimes the more experienced partner is embarrassed to show what he or she knows, so make an agreement that you will not judge them for their past sexual experiences.

Inhibitions and Embarrassment. It is usually people who were brought up with very strict prohibitions against sexual expression who have the most difficulty enjoying sex on either the giving or receiving end. An inhibited person may express disgust if certain sexual practices, or dislike the sounds, smells, and touch of another person's body. Sex isn't dirty just in the mental sense, but in the physical sense.

An inhibited person sees sex as gross and unnecessary. They may express a feeling of being above wanting to experience sexual pleasure. It is as if by denying their sexuality, they become purer somehow than the rest of humanity. Of course, the sad fact is that they are the ones losing out on one of life's great experiences.

Related to inhibition is embarrassment. If being inhibited means disliking the sensual experience of a partner's body, then embarrassment has to do with discomfort over one's own body and / or sexual function.

For example, sometimes women are afraid of losing continence, or urinating, if they have orgasm. Men may be afraid that they can't sustain a position that is uncomfortable, even though their partner may enjoy it. In other words, people like to maintain as much control in the bedroom as they do in the living room.

The thing is, of course, that bodies are made of

flesh and blood; we aren't machines. Things happen. Muscles cramp, and people sweat, groan, squeak, and so on. When you are trying to be passionate, that's no time to get hung up on whether such behaviors are appropriate or not. Best to accept evidence of bodily functions. Pay more attention to what appeals to you and less to that which does not.

Shame and Guilt. Shame and guilt probably create more sad bedroom scenes than any other feeling. Shame and guilt come from many sources, including parents, religious upbringing, and past negative sexual experiences, such as being molested or date raped.

Shame and guilt do differ from one another. Shame is what you feel when you are made to feel like something about you is wrong or bad. For example, you may have felt shame because a parent caught you masturbating. Masturbation is a natural behavior, but because your parent shamed you for it, you generalized that other sexual urges were wrong, too.

Guilt is normal and even healthy when you have done something you shouldn't have; you can frequently test out healthy guilt if you ask yourself if anyone would feel guilty if they had done the same thing. Guilt is unhealthy when you haven't done anything wrong, but feel bad anyway. A common example, unfortunately, is when someone is molested and feels guilty for having participated in sexual activity.

But you don't have to have had something really awful happen to you to feel guilty. For instance, as Americans we are drilled that we have to work hard, much as our Puritan ancestors did. With such a strong work ethic, many people feel guilty making time strictly for pleasure.

Or you may have had well-meaning parents whose sex education plan for you was to tell you only the bad parts of getting sexually involved, namely unplanned pregnancy or a disease. It's hard to imagine not having a sense of doing something "wrong," then, once you do become sexually active. And if by chance you do experience one of the unfortunate outcomes of sex, your guilt will only be multiplied.

Shame and guilt can take up a mighty big amount of space in your brain where you have "sex" filed. You can almost guarantee that you will spoil your sexual pleasure when you have these two passion killers on your mind.

Being Mechanical. Sex can become mechanical for the reasons I've just examined. Bad feelings about sex can make you feel stilted and unnatural when it comes time to make love. The irony is that so many couples say that one of the reasons they enjoy having sex with one another is to feel "connected."

Sex also becomes clumsy when you lack confidence. If you are thinking more about your next move than what gives you and your partner pleasure, you're going to end up not pleasing either one of you.

Most of all, sex can become mechanical when it occurs without emotion. Even couples that have been together a long time and who love one another can find themselves feeling empty after having sex when feelings are unexpressed.

Sometimes people try to make up for a lack of emotional expression with great technique. It isn't unusual, when a client is solo in my office, to talk about his or her great lovemaking skill. Obviously, physical skill is important, or I wouldn't have devoted half my book to that topic.

But being able to show someone how you feel about them through lovemaking is also a skill. Think of it as an emotional or relationship skill. When you express emotion while making love, you have the opportunity to experience real intimacy. Looking into one another's eyes, gently caressing one another's body, or holding hands at the peak of ecstasy are all simple but wonderful ways to strengthen the loving bond you want to have with one another.

Perhaps it's because movies and television

portray an emotional connection as being very lusty. However, passion comes in many forms.

A languid but meaningful lovemaking session may have more meaning than one with a lot of quick grinding and loud groaning. Passion is not just measured by the quality of your climax. Passion is a feeling, not an activity.

Tom's Story

When I made love to a woman in the past, I prided myself on being a good lover, or at least what I thought was a good lover. I had all kinds of little tricky maneuvers, like I knew just how to nuzzle a woman's ears to make her gasp. And I was absolutely the magician when it came to giving oral sex!

Then I met Jill. She was awesomely beautiful, but had grown up in a very conservative culture. She didn't mind having her ears nuzzled, though it didn't make her gasp. But she hated oral sex! She said that she found it "lacked intimacy."

I couldn't even figure out what she was talking about. Being there, close to her like that, was about as intimate as I thought I could be.

Then she explained that she liked having my face close to her face, because she liked looking into my eyes. This was really new to me, because I had always kept my eyes pretty much closed when I had sex.

So we made love with our eyes open as we kissed and touched one another. It was weird because it was kind of uncomfortable, I can only explain it as feeling too close. But since I really loved Jill, I stayed with the experience. My getting that close to Jill made her very aroused, and that turned me on much more than giving oral sex to any woman had ever done.

That's when I figured out the difference between having sex and making love. When I used my oral sex technique on Jill, it didn't mean much to her emotionally, and sex didn't have meaning. But when we slowed things down and literally saw each other eye to eye, we really expressed our feelings.

Making love the way we did changed my feelings about sex and love. I could see us making love this way until we grew old together, which was very cool.

It isn't that I stopped enjoying giving oral sex; it's just that technique is now only a part of my sexual experience with Jill, who is learning to relax and enjoy it, too. I guess seeing each other, looking into each other's hearts, made her trust me more so that I could show her some new ways to enjoy sex. It's like we have the best of both worlds.

If you think about it, a confident lover is a passionate lover. What is passion, after all, but an all-encompassing interest in something outside of you? Show your partner caring, and you'll generate passion in your relationship, both in and out of the bedroom.

Chapter 4

4. Why are You Having Sex, Anyway?

One of the ways to make sex more passionate is to understand why you are showing up to make love in the first place. If you don't understand what sex means to you, it may just come to feel like a chore or an obligation. Or if you show up for sport, you may find that you are missing out on some of the other benefits of sex. (And, more than likely, your partner will point that out to you, as well!)

People have sex for different reasons, because it means something different to each person. People find that sex...

- Feels great

- Helps them to connect to their partner

- Eases muscle aches and pains

- Improves their mood

- Dissolves emotional tension

- Compensates for some of the negatives of a committed relationship (e.g., sacrificing is easier when you have good sex)

- Celebrates the spiritual aspects of joining together as one

- Bonds a couple together

- Makes their relationship different from a friendship

- Gives them something to look forward to

- Creates a feeling of intimacy

- Allows an expression of loving feelings

What about you? Have you ever really thought about what having sex means to you? Or your partner?

Sometimes assumptions are made. One partner thinks that the other shows up for sex just to feel good, when in fact their partner finds sex a true act of love. Another may show up for a spiritual celebration, while their partner is looking for a sleep sedative.

Try something: Write down whatever statements ring true for you, and then put down why that is so. Invite your partner to do the same. And talk about it.

In fact, this is a great topic to get started in talking about sex in a healthy way. It doesn't matter that you show up for different reasons--what matters is that you talk about it. Then you can decide how you can both get your sexual needs met in the best possible way.

For example, if one of you likes sex because it is relaxing, and the other because it is loving, the loving partner can give the relaxing partner a massage, and the relaxing partner can whisper sweet nothings to the loving partner. Or you can trade off who's going to do what to whom. Or you might have several different needs. Great! You can now let your partner know what sex means to you and create an experience that you really find fulfilling.

The point is that so far in this book you have been on a journey of discovery about your sexuality. Face it, pretty much no one talks about sex in a healthy way. It's a topic that's either neglected or presented in negative terms.

Time to grow up, to learn about and express your sexual self on your own terms. Time to make love like an adult, with full passion and enjoyment.

Why Does Passion Fade?

Almost every couple in my office wants to know why the passion they initially felt for one another faded away like a piece of colored paper left out in the sun. After all, people often judge whether they have found their soul mate by how good a sexual connection they have.

Unfortunately, this should not be the only criterion for picking a partner, mainly because when passion does fade, people worry terribly that perhaps they made a mistake when they picked their partner after all.

But it may not mean that after all, as passion fades naturally for nearly every couple. And it's nothing to worry about, if you know what happened and how to make sex exciting once again.

Sex, Love, and the Mind

So what does happen? First of all, when you met your partner, you matched him or her to what sexologist John Money called a "love map." Think of a love map as a model kept in your brain that can lead you to the kind of person that turns you on, first physically, and later emotionally and intellectually.

There are many powerful factors that go into the creation of this love map. Some elements include qualities that you admire in people around you, including family members, teachers, peers, and even celebrities.

Others are biologically driven, such as finding a partner that looks healthy and vital enough to be your mate in a multitude of areas, such as work and parenting. And still more factors are social, such as meeting a partner whom your parents might approve of, or who shares the same religious beliefs.

So, from a psychological point of view, rather than looking for a real, live human being, you are looking for an ideal.

An ideal is a fantasy. You project this fantasy onto a person who seems to come close to all the elements you created in your love map. Think of projecting a fantasy this way: You have a transparent, ideal person that you place over the real person who is before you. On one level, you know that there is a real person there; on another, you only want to see your fantasy.

So you deny, or fail to see, the flaws in your chosen partner. The problem is, you can't keep this fantasy up forever. The real partner, after all, has his or her own needs and wants, his or her own personality. Your chosen partner doesn't exist simply to make you happy.

You begin to see the flaws and get disappointed. And, as you might imagine, some of those flaws are in the bedroom department. Whereas once upon a time you could overlook a little bit of a potbelly, now it starts to bother you. Or that funny groan that your partner makes at orgasm no longer seems so cute. And the inhibitions, such as not wanting to try oral sex or even a new position, become simply frustrating.

From a psychological standpoint, your ideal is shattered. Now you have a tough task: Figuring out how to make love to someone that is simply human.

The Biology of Sex and Love

When you met a potential mate that matched up to your love map, all kinds of brain chemicals popped and fizzed. One of those chemicals, dopamine, is a so-called "reward chemical." When you have sex with someone that makes you feel good, dopamine increases, and you want to do it all over again.

Endorphins are another "happy chemical" that get released. Endorphins are natural painkillers, so sex really does make you feel better in mind and body. "Cuddle chemicals" like oxytocin (ox-e-toe-sin) and vasopressin (vase-oh-press-in) are also released in the brain. These chemicals cause you to feel bonded to your partner.

Becoming attached to your partner is a wonderful thing, isn't it? According to anthropologists like Helen Fisher, from an evolutionary point of view makes it more likely that couples will stay together if they become pregnant. Having a mate stick around and take care of you through thick and thin, or to build a more secure financial future together are also benefits of being a bonded couple.

And besides, Mother Nature isn't going to let you stay gaga forever. You have other stuff you have to do to survive that have nothing to do with sex. You know, shop for groceries. Do the laundry. Go to the job. Call your aunt. You simply have to leave the bedroom sometime and take care of the business of life!

Unfortunately, what often happens is that life takes over, and sex becomes less and less of a priority. When you hear the cliché that "you need to work on your marriage," that includes sex. You can't just expect sexual passion to sweep you up after a day of cleaning up kitty hairballs or yelling at someone on the phone at work. Nor can you make time for sex if you fill your life to the very brim with other activities.

Your Relationship, Sex, and Love

It's no secret that passion can fade because of problems in your relationship. Too often, couples try to treat sex as something that is separate from every other aspect of the relationship. The partner who is sarcastic and critical by day may still expect a sensual lovemaking session by night. The partner who has been largely absent due to work wants sexual attention. The partner who is dull expects to be entertained in bed.

If you want to have passionate lovemaking sessions, you're going to have to think like lovers. That doesn't mean just patting each other's po-po's as you step out of the shower, then sending a dirty little text, followed by footsy under the dining table at night.

What it does mean is cherishing one another. To cherish means to hold dear, to show affection for someone. If you cherish someone, would you criticize his or her every move? Demand that they do things your way? Roll your eyes every time they open their mouth to speak?

Occasionally I have a wise person in my office that understands that if you want to make love at night, you have to start in the morning. Your partner is the person you adore; show it. Sweet gestures, a kind tone of voice, and care taken when giving feedback will go a long way toward creating an atmosphere of trust and intimacy.

Think about your own attitude toward your partner. Do you truly act in a way that would make your partner want you?

Or are you . . .?

- prickly

- grumpy

- sullen

- bitchy

- irritable

- regretful

What if, instead, you adopted some more attractive qualities, such as . . .?

- caring

- supportive

- empathic

- warm

- humorous

- generous

- sensitive

Wouldn't you want to get into bed and make sweet love to someone who treated you well? How can you expect passion to last if you both are dumping relationship cold water on the warm fires of love every day? (Sorry for the stretched metaphor!)

You can try all the techniques in the universe to get your partner turned on, but if your daily behavior is a turn off, you can forget about making your partner squirm against your own body when you get into bed.

Sexual Connection

Learning how to receive pleasure is as important as giving pleasure to your partner. In our hurry-up culture, it is easier to be in the do-er role. A person who is always doing something may be trying to distract themselves from paying attention to their own needs and wants by paying attention to someone (or something) else.

That can be true even when it comes to sex. Sex

makes some people feel nervous, so if they can be the one giving pleasure, it can help them feel more in control. This may be helpful to your partner, but you are also doing a dozen other things of which you may not be aware.

When you are always the giver, you lose your own focus and don't get the chance to experience all the pleasure that you might. Sex might become dull, or you might even feel resentful after awhile.

The other thing that happens is you miss out on intimacy. If you are rarely the receiver, then you aren't giving your partner a chance to know you sexually--at the deepest, most intimate level.

If you tend to be the giver, maybe it's time to try switching roles. Find out what it is like to have little or no responsibility except to let your partner know what you prefer, what makes you feel good. Appreciate, too, that it may take a little courage to tell your partner what you like. And it may take getting used to laying back and taking it all in.

What if you are the partner who is always receiving? Being the receiver can also let you hide a part of your sexuality, a part that may like to be given expression. Putting yourself in the role of giver allows you to experiment with being more aggressive or creative. You also get the chance to know what turns your partner on, and what it is like to build on your partner's responses to you.

You don't have to keep switching roles every time you make love, or worse, keep score. Just by noticing your role, you can check in with yourself to see what it is that you need or want, both from yourself and your partner.

PART TWO:
Physical Passion

Chapter 5

5. The Body Sexual

In this part of the book, the focus is on bodily pleasure. If you skipped Part I, I urge you to go back and read it. After all, in a long-term relationship, creating and re-creating passionate sex depends on the emotional tone and trust level between the two of you.

To experience the best physical pleasure, you need to understand:

Sexual anatomy: Your "pleasure map"

Body image: Loving your own body

Sensual exploration: Massage, fantasy, and your environment

Foreplay: The how-to of sexual arousal

Orgasm: The "pleasure peak"

After play: Keeping the warmth in your passionate connection

As you read this section, it's fine to let your mind wander a bit. Imagine what you can do with this knowledge! In fact, in the old, old days, having sex with someone was called "knowing" him or her.

And all this time, you thought sex education was "just say no!"

Body Image

While most people feel good or neutral about their bodies, an amazing percentage of people feel bad, awkward, ashamed, or squeamish about their physical being.

Jamie: *My husband tells me that he loves my body, but I have no idea what he's talking about. I'm just a torso with some sticks!*

Isabelle: *I can't stand to have my partner give me oral sex. I absolutely hate it when he looks at me "down there."*

Len: *I know it's dumb, but my wife had a lot of partners before we got married. I worry that I just don't "measure up" to them.*

Greta: *I can't stand how sex smells, even saliva. I don't want to smell my own odor, let alone my partner's.*

Such attitudes don't develop in a vacuum. It takes training and experience, usually by parents who also feel bad about their bodies, or through religious teachings, to learn to hate one's own body, or their partner's body.

I can almost guarantee that once upon a time, you ran your hands over your body, and it felt good. You may have discovered your body while you were taking a bath or a shower, or while you were changing your clothing.

You also may have noticed how good your body felt when your mom or dad held you on their lap or gave you a hug. You liked being touched, and thought it was fine to touch yourself, too.

Then, you may have found your genitals. And that's when the fun may have stopped. You may have gotten caught. Perhaps you got a shameful lecture, or a sharp, "Don't do that! That's disgusting!"

Or you may have noticed that touching your own body was an activity no one ever talked about, just like sex, so it might not be a nice thing to do. You knew it felt good to touch yourself, but it seemed off limits, so you refrained. Touching your body became a source of embarrassment and shame.

If those early experiences weren't enough to confuse you, your body changed as you entered puberty. Suddenly, the appearance of pubic hair and other secondary characteristics announced to the world that your body was preparing for reproduction--and sex. But instead of celebrating, you may have been teased by your family and friends.

For many children, your body, once a source of pleasure, now became a burden. And it isn't just women, either, who worry. Men can also become guilty about the sexual pleasure they feel with their bodies.

Yes, some of the deepest, darkest fears that people experience in bed have to do with their own bodies. Silly fears. Fears that keep them from enjoying sex.

Fears that keep them from enjoying sex? Maybe that's the point! Maybe if they weren't so uptight about this body part or that body function, they'd enjoy themselves...and then they would really feel bad!

But it's your body, no one else's, so you might as well get reacquainted with it. The way you feel about your body is fundamental to your enjoyment of sex.

Before Knowing Your Partner, Know Yourself

The first step is to just become comfortable being in your own skin. I have spoken with clients who are so uncomfortable with and ashamed of their own bodies that they cannot appear nude to their partner after a shower. They change in the closet. They must make love in the dark.

The human body is a thing of beauty. It is why Michelangelo sculpted the body, both male and female, in his fantastic marbles, why Titian painted his glorious nudes, why Edward Weston chose it as a primary photographic subject. In fact, Weston's secondary subject was nature; what does that say about the beauty of the human form?

When you hide your body from your partner, you are depriving him or her of enjoying its delights. At the same time, you stay behind a veil of shame, depriving yourself of the chance not just to feel proud, but also to experience the feeling of being physically aroused. I don't just mean sexually aroused, I mean *alive!*

You can start becoming more comfortable with your body by celebrating it as a source of pleasure and wonder--wonder because of its ability to do so many amazing things to keep you attune with your environment and help you--and our species--to survive. Wonder because it has the ability to reproduce offspring. Wonder because of the way it takes care of you, all automatically, without a thought.

All that being said, I frequently work with men and women whose sexuality has been challenged by illnesses like cancer. Bodies do change. They falter and disappoint both its owner and his or her partner. So I've included in the following section some ideas for people whose body complaints are more than just "all in your head."

Introducing You to Yourself

When you are stuck in your attitude—about anything, really—sometimes doing something concrete can help you make a change. In fact, sex therapy clients in my office frequently ask for "homework assignments". I often make up such assignments on the spot, creating them to help the client both think about their own behavior and to move toward their goals.

The activities that I have included here are designed to help you have a more positive outlook toward your own body. Once you have comfort within your own skin, you can modify the activities to change the way you think about your partner's body as well.

Take your time with each exercise, and don't be afraid to go back and repeat as needed to create comfort with your body.

Focus on What's Right

If you have negative thoughts about your body, try keeping a daily gratitude list specifically for all the things that your body does *right*. This activity can be useful whether or not your body is in perfect health. Pay attention to what your body does for you, and write it down. Start with things that happen outside the bedroom. Your list might look like this:

- I am able to walk where I need to go.

- My ears let me hear the sound of our cats purring

- I used my hands to trim back my rose bushes.

- Continue until you start to appreciate your body overall.

Then, take it to another level by noticing, appreciating, and listing those things about your body that are more sexual in nature. My guess is that if you haven't been sexually confident about your body, you've ignored some important details such as these:

- My lips allow me to express my love with a kiss.

- I love to feel my partner's thigh beneath my hand when we sit side by side.

- I like the way my skin feels when my silk blouse rubs against it.

You get the idea. As you pay more attention, add more sexual details such as how your genitals tingle to let you know that you are aroused, or how much you appreciate the way your hands can caress your partner's breasts.

The secret, then, to enjoying your body is valuing what it does, rather than mourning what does not. Very few people have a perfect body, and even those that do may not appreciate it the way that you think they might.

Focus on the positive, and see if you don't change your attitude toward the body, both yours and your partner's.

Use a Mirror Exercise

Mirror exercises are frequently used in therapy with people who are diagnosed with eating disorders or a condition known as *body dysmorphic disorder* (BDD). People who are diagnosed with BDD do not see their bodies accurately. For example, a man with perfectly adequate abdominal muscles may see flab, or a woman with a nose that would be considered normal sees it as large and unattractive.

Of course, with our country's current craze for physical perfection, with millions and millions of dollars spent on cosmetic surgery and other procedures every year, it isn't surprising that many people have at least some of the symptoms of BDD.

To use the mirror as a helper in getting you to be more comfortable with your body, start by standing in front of a full-length mirror with your clothing on. Let your eyes scan lightly over your whole image in the mirror. Maintain an accepting, loving attitude toward yourself as you scan again, this time, looking for anything about your face or body that you like. Say aloud to yourself, "I like my hands" or "I have beautiful eyes".

Do NOT permit yourself to stare at parts of your body that are less than appealing to you. Do NOT criticize your body in any way. Just stay focused on what you like.

Spend only a few minutes in front of the mirror in order to do this exercise. If you are a "checker," stop checking your image except when you do this exercise or to evaluate your outfit when you get dressed in the morning. Repeat until you start to notice your positive qualities in the mirror right away.

Like the gratitude list described above, the next step would be to do the exercise again unclothed. If this is too overwhelming for you, then try looking at yourself unclothed from the waist up or waist down to start. Again, notice only what you like. If this is difficult, think about things like your skin color, its smoothness, the outline of a muscle, the color or curl of your hair, or whatever.

Do NOT let yourself spend any more time than is necessary to notice what you like. The moment you become critical of yourself, step away from the mirror.

What if you really do have flaws, like scars or moles, creases or wrinkles? Turn to page 62 to find out more about accepting, or perhaps changing, your body.

The Joy of Nudity

Sometime ago, I researched and wrote an encyclopedia article on nudity. Of all the things that signal shame about the human body, clothing must be number one on the list. Unless you live in a climate where you must protect yourself or risk death, there isn't much reason a lot of the time to wear clothing. But in fact, just appearing nude in the street could get you arrested most anywhere in the United States.

Our ideas about the unclothed body can be downright prudish. That's why I think it's important to spend time naked. That's right, naked. Spend some time nude every day. I don't mean parading around in the living room with the drapes open. I mean that when you get out of the shower don't be in such a rush to put on clothing. After you make love, enjoy resting and relaxing in the nude. Maybe pull the blinds closed and enjoy being in a room in the flesh.

Be a little European and casual about nudity so that you are more comfortable with your body when it comes time to disrobe for lovemaking.

Bodies Do Differ

What if there is something truly different about your body?

For example, your body may have developed to be lopsided, or became disfigured by illness or surgery, or have some unattractive, quirky feature. (On my feet, my fourth toe is longer than my third toe; no surgery is ever going to correct that, and so I must walk the earth with a toe sticking out over the edge of my sandals.)

You may have scars from surgeries or burns, blemishes and blotches from the sun, or more or less hair than you'd like, in places where you may or may not want hair. Wrinkles, moles, and dimples show up in unexpected places; gravity and age do their part to break down the body.

You may need to decide whether or not you want to do something about the physical feature that troubles you. You may very well decide that a tummy tuck to whisk away evidence of the 80 lbs. you lost will be worthwhile. On the other hand, for a man losing his hair, a great haircut from a new stylist may be all that's required.

Middle-ground approaches are kind of tough when you are expected to be nude. It's hard to wear a padded bra or undershirt to bed when you want to be passionate. Why not? You make the rules! Wear harem pants and carry a toy parrot on your shoulder, if that's what turns you on.

Clear communication about your body is always a good idea. If you have features about which you are sensitive, be sure to tell your partner that he or she can tease you about your Don King hairdo in the morning, but not your blemish that's shaped exactly like Idaho.

Complaining about your body is a sexual turnoff— a passion killer! If you are disfigured or disabled by your body, then talking to your doctor and/or a therapist may help you cope. Bring your partner along for support. You may find out that they don't really notice, or if they do, they're perfectly okay with it.

The Importance of Touch

It's unusual, of course, to withdraw from touch. We have "skin hunger," or the desire to be caressed and held. Babies who do not receive touch may fail to thrive. Touch is one of the first ways in which humans communicate caring to a newborn infant.

When someone doesn't care to be touched, one of several things may have happened:

- Failure to receive enough touch as a baby or small child, sometimes due to a mother's depression.

- Physical or emotional abuse, causing a person to become withdrawn.

- Physical or emotional needs neglected, causing a person to stop caring or trusting.

- Sexual abuse or exposure to inappropriate sexual behavior, causing a person to become guarded.

Sometimes a person who doesn't like touch has a problem with cleanliness and is afraid of actual contact with another person, or is turned off by odors, perspiration, and so on.

You can overcome this problem, but it will take time, as well as patience on the part of your partner. You will need to communicate with your partner about your desire to develop trust. Go slowly, make eye contact if you can, and let your partner know where your "edge"--the place beyond your comfort zone--lies.

Little by little, try to expand your comfort zone until you feel okay being touched almost anywhere on your body. (You may always have sensitive places that you want left alone, say a place behind your ear. A gentle reminder will let your lover know to stay within your [hopefully expanded] comfort zone.)

Be sure to reflect on the questions asked about your sexual development at the beginning of this book; discuss them with your partner.

Take the lovemaking suggestions in this E-book in small steps. After all, you have the rest of your life to understand and explore your sexuality. And consider seeing a therapist (see Resources) to help you enjoy touch.

Another way to enjoy touch safely is with massage. You can find many books and DVDs on this topic. Sometimes community colleges or other settings offer classes for couples to take.

Sex and Your Health

Of course, there are some things you do have control over. Flab from lack of exercise or rolls of fat from a poor diet are things that you can change about yourself. Get a good book on nutrition or make an appointment with a dietitian. Get a personal trainer, join a gym, or buy a sturdy pair of walking shoes. (Note: Be sure to get a physical before making any diet or exercise changes. You also want to rule out any medical reasons for extra weight, such as thyroid disorders.)

Not only will proper diet and regular exercise improve the way you look, but it will also help you sexually in other ways. You'll have more energy, more stamina, and have more balanced hormones.

Keeping yourself attractive isn't just to make your partner happy; it's also to keep you healthy and vital as long as possible. As you might guess, this is yet another secret of passion, keeping yourself fit for sex.

Chapter 6

6. Sexual Anatomy

Partners that stay passionate cherish one another's bodies. A woman understands her lover's penis isn't just a shaft of flesh; it is a magnificent structure, with detail and purpose. A man understands his lover's vulva isn't just folds of tissue surrounding an orifice (opening); it is a beautiful flower of sensitive tissue beckoning him to enter his partner's vagina, the most intimate and treasured part of her body.

The following section is intended not just to help you have a basic understanding of the body when engaged in sexual activity, but also how to apply what you know for better sex. Just because you *think* you know what you're looking at, you may not be aware of all the intricacies—the little details—of your own or your partner's body.

Once again, please don't skip over this section because it looks like a boring old science lesson from high school. There is value in studying a drawing so that you can apply loving touch to your partner's sexual anatomy.

Plus, a lot of folks don't know what's what

especially when it comes to women. Not only are women's genitals more cleverly hidden from view than are men's, but women are not socialized to explore themselves.

While I was writing this book, Dr. Laura Berman was on "Oprah" showing a gigantic drawing of the female genitals and using a pointer to show women the exact location of the clitoris. Yes, there really are women who do not know how to find this little pearl of pleasure on their own bodies. You or your partner may be one of them. You have a choice to remedy that, or remain in the closet about a woman's remarkable sexual anatomy.

But such physical ignorance isn't limited to women. It is only in the last decade or so that scientists really understand the mechanism of the male erection. Because pharmaceutical companies were gung-ho on finding a medical solution to erectile dysfunction (ED), they needed to learn all about the complex system of blood circulation and engorgement in the penis.

While the drawings are generic, it's important to remember that everyone's body is different. Just because one man finds it exquisite to have his perineum stroked, doesn't mean every man does. (If you don't know what the *perineum* is, see below!) The fact is that most people come into marriage or committed relationship having had other partners. I have had people in my office take things quite personally when their trademark "move" that always worked for previous partners doesn't work for the one they love most.

So you need to be flexible in your approach to one another's bodies. Learning how your partner's body is both the same and unique from other people's bodies is part of the fun of exploration, and part of what helps you continue to create passionate sex that brings you satisfaction and contentment.

Men's Bodies, Explained

Let's start with the most basic of sexual basics, the genitals. Here is a drawing of a man's sexual reproductive system.

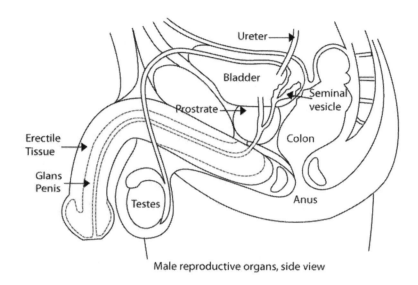

Male reproductive organs, side view

And here is what they are.

Penis. When a man becomes aroused, his brain signals the *corpora cavernosa*, which are tube-like structures in the penis, to produce nitrous oxide. This leads to the creation of chemical that causes the arteries of the penis to dilate or open.

Pressurized blood can then enter the penis quickly. The pressurized blood is held in the penis when veins leaving the penis constrict or close in another chemical process.

The blood is then trapped in the *corpus cavernosa*, which are tubular structures within the penis. This makes the penis elongate and become stiff.

If the arteries leading to the penis do not open properly, this can lead to impotence or erectile dysfunction.

Ejaculation of semen and orgasm occur with enough sexual stimulation. Ejaculation is accompanied by the rhythmic contractions of orgasm that last on average about 17 seconds.

You may be surprised to learn that in fact ejaculation and orgasm are two different events. A man can have orgasm without ejaculation, but almost never will he have ejaculation without orgasm. This is the reason that, with much practice, men can learn to have multiple orgasms.

Glans or Head. The *glans*, or head, of the penis is very sensitive, as it is the endpoint of many nerves. If a man is uncircumcised, a thin membrane of skin called the foreskin or prepuce covers the glans. When an uncircumcised man has an erection, the foreskin pulls back to reveal the glans. During intercourse or other sex play, the foreskin moves up and down over the glans. The amount of pleasure a man experiences is not dependent on whether his foreskin is intact.

The *meatus*, or urethral opening, is in the center of glans and has the shape of a slit.

Shaft. The shaft of the penis contains spongy tissue that helps the penis become stiff. This tissue is shaped as three cylinders. The *corpus spongiosum* is found on the underside of the penis; it expands at one end to form the glans. The corpus spongiosum surrounds the urethra and compresses it when the penis is erect, so urine cannot pass out of the penis when a man is hard, only semen. The other two cylinders, the corpora cavernosa, are on the topside of the penis.

When a man has an erection, it means that these three cylinders have become engorged with blood. The corpus spongiosum and the corpora cavernosa extend into the body toward the anus, underneath the prostate gland, to form the base of the penis. The root of the penis is kept in place with ligaments.

Urethra. The urethra carries both urine and sperm through the penis. There is a sphincter muscle that contracts to allow either urine or semen down the urethra, but not both at once.

Frenulum. This is the area on the underside of the penis where the head meets the shaft. The skin here is puckered, and it holds the foreskin to the head. It is a sensitive area and the majority of men like attention here during lovemaking.

Corona. Corona literally means "crown." On the penis, the corona is the ridge around the base of the glans where it meets the shaft. It is sensitive to pressure; this is the area where a man may try a squeeze during lovemaking to last longer until orgasm.

Testicles. The testicles, or testes, are extremely sensitive. The testicles are contained in the sac-like structure known as the *scrotum*. The scrotum helps keep control the temperature of the testicles for sperm production. When the testicles are warm, the scrotum will hang lower to act as "air conditioning". Amazingly, each testicle produces almost 150 million sperm every 24 hours.

The testicles also produce male hormones, or androgens, including testosterone. Testosterone is responsible for a man's drive or *libido*, the amount of body hair he has, muscularity and tone, and stamina.

Perineum. This is sensitive skin that covers the area between the anus and testicles. It may seem like a flat, barren area, but men find it pleasurable to have the perineum stimulated.

Anus: The orifice through which the feces are expelled. The anus actually has a lot of nerve endings and some men enjoy anal stimulation. Please note, straight men like anal stimulation, too. (See "Prostate," below.)

Internal Sex Organs

Here is a drawing of a man's internal sex organs.

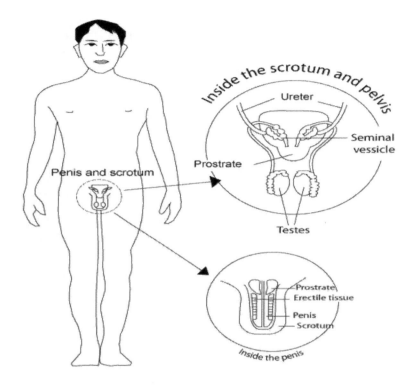

And here is what they are.

Vas Deferens. The vas deferens is ducts that take the sperm from each testicle to the penis. The vas deferens has no other function, so this is the area that is surgically cut if a man has a vasectomy.

Seminal vesicles. These are the glands that release seminal fluid, which makes up about two-thirds of the substance in semen. Seminal fluid contains fructose, which provides energy for the sperm during their journey, and *prostaglandins* that help break down the mucous lining of the cervix so that the sperm can enter the uterus more easily.

Bulbourethral glands. These glands release the pre-seminal fluid that is seen at the tip of the penis before orgasm. This fluid keeps the ph balance just right for the sperm.

Prostate gland. This small gland creates about a quarter of the fluid contained in semen. If stimulated, it may cause an intense orgasm. The prostate can be manipulated by feeling a finger, or fingers, into the anus.

Pubococcegeus muscle. Also known as the "PC" muscle, it supports the pelvic floor and is responsible for the powerful contractions felt during orgasm. Men as well as women need to keep the PC muscle in good tone. To exercise this muscle, first you need to find it. When urinating, stop midstream. The muscle you use to do that is your PC muscle. You can tense and relax this muscle for a set of 10 a couple of times a day.

Women's Bodies, Explained

External Sex Organs

The female reproductive system is as complex as a man's, but fluctuating hormones can cause physiological and psychological changes that men do not experience. Here are a basic drawing of the woman's external genitalia:

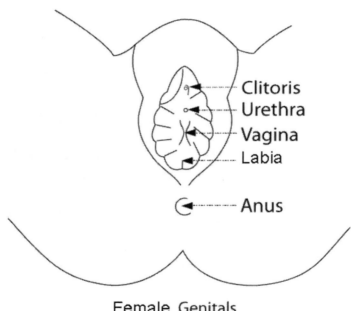

Female Genitals

Here is what they are.

Labia. The vulva is the outside part of the female genitals that are visible to the eye. The *labia majora*, or outside labia, are covered with pubic hair. The inner labia, or *labia minora*, are thinner and less fleshy. They are more sensitive to stimulation.

Every woman's labia are different in appearance; on some women, the labia minora are hidden, on other women, the labia protrude from the labia majora.

Mons Pubis. This is the mound of fatty tissue that protects the pubic bone during intercourse. The mons is covered with pubic hair.

Clitoris. The clitoris is the small organ that peeps out when the labia minora and hood are pulled away. It has many nerve endings, and is the only organ in either male or female bodies that exists solely for pleasure. The clitoris extends far into the female body; some researchers think that it is connected to the vagina at the *G-spot* (see below).

At the tip of the clitoris is the *glans*, which sits atop the shaft. The glans, shaft, and surrounding structures are made of erectile tissue. When a woman is excited or stimulated, the clitoris becomes engorged. Direct stimulation to the clitoris is almost always uncomfortable; it is better to stimulate the hood over the clitoris for the most pleasure.

Urethral Opening. The urethra is a very small opening just below the clitoris. The *hymen*, a thin membrane of skin, covers the urethral opening and part of the vaginal opening, leaving room for menstrual blood and other fluids to exit. The hymen is often thought to be broken at first vaginal intercourse, but in fact it is usually torn with the use of tampons or vigorous exercise.

Perineum. This is the area between the bottom of the entrance of a woman's vagina and the anus. It has many nerve endings; for that reason some women like this area to be rubbed or massaged.

Anus. This is the tight opening to the rectum. It, too, has many nerve endings. Some women like to have anal play as part of lovemaking. It is important to wash anything--fingers, toys, or penis--that enters the anus before it enters the vagina.

And also there are:

Breasts. The breasts are comprised of a mass of *milk gland tissue* surrounded by fat. The *milk ducts* from the glands lead to an area called the *milk sinus*, which is just behind the nipple. Tissue that is fibrous lies between the ducts, which are what gives breasts their firmness and shape. Breasts naturally vary in size; the amount of pleasure a woman feels when her breasts are caressed has no correlation to size.

Nipples. Only the little bud that protrudes from the center of the pigmented area on a woman's breast is actually the nipple. The colored area surrounding the nipple is called the *aureola*. The color of the aureola depends on a woman's skin color. Size varies from woman to woman. The little nodes scattered on the surface of the areola are the *tubercles of Montgomery* (now there's a sexy term!) and are normal.

On both men and women, the nipples are one of the most sensitive areas. Some women are able to have orgasm by stimulation to the nipples alone. However, some women find stimulation to the nipples to be uncomfortable, so you need to check this with your partner.

Internal Sex Organs

Here are drawings of the female sex organs:

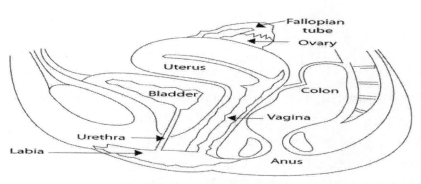

Female Pelvis, Side View

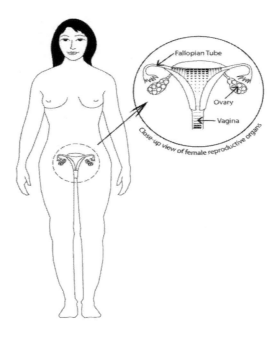

Here is what they are:

Vagina. The word *vagina* translates from Latin as meaning "sheath," and that is one purpose of this organ, which is to act as a sheath to surround the penis during intercourse. Of course, it is also the birth passage. As such, the vagina is a very stretchy organ.

During arousal, the vagina lengthens and balloons to accommodate the penis; during birth, it needs to expand enough in diameter to accommodate an infant's head as it passes down the birth canal.

The vagina has its own system for cleansing itself and keeping the environment at the correct ph balance to prevent the overgrowth of bacteria like yeast. It is unnecessary to douche, and only water- or silicone-based lubricants should be used during intercourse.

The amount of lubrication produced by the vagina during arousal varies from woman to woman. For some women, there is increased dryness as they approach the age of menopause. Lubrication may depend on where a woman is in her menstrual cycle, or even her stress level. For that reason, it is a good idea to always have on hand and use a lubricant during intercourse.

G-Spot. The G-spot is short for the "Graffenberg spot," named after the physician who first identified this structure. The G-spot lies within a woman's vagina, about 1-1/2" to 2" from the entrance on the top side. The purpose of the G-spot is uncertain. Some women find stimulation to the G-spot pleasurable while others do not.

Cervix. The cervix is a bottleneck-like structure that connects the uterus, or womb, to the vagina. To help sperm travel to the uterus, the cervix drops down during intercourse. Some women can feel the penis against the cervix during intercourse. Of those women, some find it pleasure and others do not; for those that do not, using positions that discourage deep thrusting, such as scissors (see page 150) are preferred.

Uterus. The uterus is also called the womb, the place where the egg is fertilized by sperm, develops into an embryo, then a fetus, and finally a full-term infant.

The uterus is made up of layers of tissue and muscle.

Each month, the inner lining, or endometrius, of the uterus builds up in preparation for the possible implantation of a fertilized egg; if no such event takes place, the lining is shed, causing menstruation. Orgasm causes contractions in the uterus, which some women find particularly pleasurable.

Fallopian Tubes. The fallopian tubes go from the ovaries to the uterus. They have protrusions at one end that are designed to pick up an egg from the ovary before the tube draws the egg into the uterus. If the egg is fertilized, the first stage of embryo development takes place within the fallopian tube.

Ovaries. The two ovaries are small, almond-shaped organs that each contain about 100,000 eggs. Each month, only one egg from one ovary is released during ovulation for possible fertilization. The ovaries also release estrogen and progesterone, which regulate the menstrual cycle.

Pelvic Floor Muscle. Also known as the pubococcygeus ("PC") muscle, this powerful muscle supports the uterus and other reproductive organs. It is also responsible for keeping the vagina in good tone. By exercising the PC muscle, you can help maintain the health of your reproductive organs. To exercise this muscle, first you need to find it. When urinating, stop midstream. The muscle you use to do that is your PC muscle. You can tense and relax this muscle for a set of

10 a couple of times a day.

Is it okay to use terms like "va-jay-jay" and "cock" to talk about private parts? Of course! And certainly you can give sweet or dirty pet names to any part you wish. Make sure of two things, however. First, use labels that are okay with your partner. If your partner hates her vulva to be called a "pussy," cross the word off your list. Second, know the real terms for your body parts so that you can talk about them with either your partner or your physician if you have a problem or question.

Chapter 7

7. Sensual Exploration of the Body

In this section, you and your partner can learn different ways to explore the world of the senses, both alone and together. Being sensual does many things for a couple trying to keep passion alive, including:

- Slowing down sex so that both of you can stay both relaxed and aroused — the real secret of great sex

- Making orgasm more likely for women, and stronger for men

- Keeping the focus on loving feelings as you nurture one another

- Providing you with endless scenarios for sexual expression and play

Sometimes it can be hard to engage in sensual exploration. Such exploration can feel intimate; not everyone is immediately comfortable with a more intense level of physical and emotional closeness.

It can be helpful to realize that there is no rush to

learn how to explore. You can take your time incorporating the ideas and suggestions that follow. I encourage you to talk about what you are learning about your own body, your partner's body, and what you like best and least about exploration.

You may decide to include sensual exploration as part of every lovemaking session, or it may happen less frequently. In a good sexual—and sensual—relationship, there should be both room for sex for the sake of sex and sex for creating a harmonious connection.

Sensual Self-Pleasure

I don't think Socrates was thinking about sex when he famously quipped, "Know thy self." But it certainly applies! Sensual exploration of your own body, especially your "erogenous zones" (sexually sensitive parts of the body) and genitals, can be an ideal way to prepare you to for communicating about your body with your partner.

In fact, when you become your own lover, a lot of wonderful things happen:

You make friends with your own body and begin to understand what kind of touch you enjoy.

You learn how to control the timing of orgasm, whether it's to slow down or make things happen a little quicker.

You become better at communicating to your partner what you like or need.

You gain confidence in yourself as you find out that you have the ability to love yourself in a wonderful way.

Now, a lot of men and women believe that masturbation is easy for men and difficult for women. That isn't necessarily so. There are both men and women that feel equally guilty about masturbation and refrain from it at all costs. Also, men are often so focused on orgasm that they do not take time to get to know other parts of their bodies.

Unless your particular religion has extreme prohibitions against self-pleasuring, there is no reason to be embarrassed or ashamed about touching your own body. Besides those benefits listed above, touching your own body has some other benefits as well. If your partner is ill or not in the mood for sex, you can still love yourself and prevent feeling resentful. If you have a higher drive than your partner, you can still have an outlet for its expression.

You may have a concern that "too much" masturbation can spoil you for your partner, draining sexual and emotional energy out of the bed you share together. Usually, it isn't self-pleasure that causes the problem, but conflict in the relationship or within the person who uses masturbation in place of sex with a partner.

If you find yourself masturbating more than seems healthy to you, then you need to take a bit of time to reflect and figure out why this is so. Try to resolve it on your own or with your partner's help, or see a sex therapist if you need assistance sorting it out.

How does self-pleasure make you a more passionate lover? When you understand how good your own body feels, it can make you eager to give that pleasure to your partner. Doesn't it make sense that pleasure begets passion?

Make Yourself Comfortable

Set the scene for your solo session just as you might for lovemaking. Straighten up the bed. Make the temperature comfortable. Light a candle. Drink a glass of wine. Put on some music. Have lubricant ready, and a towel to put beneath you if you like being a bit neat. Have some lotion nearby, too, so that you can use it on your body. While you could have toys like a vibrator available, I'd recommend that you try using your own hands for now.

Take a shower first, if it will help you to relax. (Of course, you can masturbate in the shower if that's the only private place in your life right now. Try using a water-resistant silicone lubricant, but take care in the tub or shower stall because these lubricants are slippery and they stay that way in water.)

You may want to read a romantic novel or view

some erotic DVDs or photos, or you may choose to simply concentrate on what brings you pleasure without such aids. It's entirely up to you.

Sensual Self-Knowledge for Men

The way you masturbate can affect how you act with partner. Some men masturbate as if mom was going to catch them at any second; such anxiety can add to the problem of premature ejaculation.

Other men ignore the entire rest of their bodies; with all that focus on the penis, it can lead to problems with erection. This can lead to an unfortunate "wham-bam" approach to sex that can lead to emotional dissatisfaction with your sex life later.

To create passionate sex, you want to be a sensual lover to your partner, so slow down. Take your time to learn your own body. Don't be embarrassed to explore. Pay attention to what it feels like to become aroused, and to build to orgasm.

Before you begin masturbating, use lotion or massage oil to give yourself a real massage, rubbing your arms, legs, hands, and feet in a way that feels good to you. Then caress your penis in a way that normally brings you to erection.

Continue to arouse yourself, touching yourself in places that you might normally ignore. You can play with your nipples, stimulating them with your fingers.

Or stimulate your scrotum by caressing or tapping it. Squeeze your testicles. Put pressure on the perineum. If it appeals to you, finger your anus or go further and insert a finger. And please don't worry that liking anal stimulation makes you "gay." It doesn't.

Experiment with your position during masturbation. If you are used to being prone, try kneeling or standing instead. You can also try lying on your side or even on your front, just to see how that feels or if you like a change.

Fantasy can also be a wonderful part of getting aroused. Pornography is all around, but try to experiment with something erotic instead, such as a book of beautiful photographs of nudes or other sexy but not titillating material. And what about the old-fashioned way, letting your imagination go and seeing what turns you on these days? More about fantasizing in section below.

Sensual Self-Knowledge For Women

Self-pleasure is important for the woman who wants to stay a passionate partner. After all, if you don't know what turns you on, you can't tell your partner, either. Also, many women find it easier to learn how to have an orgasm without a partner present.

Most women need time to relax in order to experience orgasm. If you've never or rarely masturbated, you should experiment and explore when you have about an hour of guaranteed private time. Don't be discouraged if you don't have an orgasm right away. You are a student of pleasure, and you need to learn just what turns you on.

If you aren't familiar with your own anatomy, you may want to begin by lying back and looking at your genitals with a mirror. Notice the hood over the clitoris, the clitoris itself, the labia or lips, and the entrance to the vagina. Now touch yourself, watching to see how what you are doing is connected to what you are feeling. Use a finger inserted into your vagina to feel how it is become lubricated or wet.

Put the mirror aside if you wish and focus on the sensations you feel as you explore your genitals. Most women prefer indirect contact on the clitoris. You can use a finger to move the hood across and / or up and down on the clitoris, or squeeze your labia gently around the clitoris and move them around. Experiment with touching your inner thighs, or cupping your hand around the mons and genitals and rubbing. Pinch or caress your nipples with your free hand to see if that makes you feel closer to orgasm.

You may come close to what feels like orgasm and then find the sensation slipping away. Don't worry about it. You are showing your body that it is okay to let go and feel pleasure.

You can choose to rest for a bit and then try some more, or allow the self-pleasuring session to end.

If having an orgasm is a new experience, once you experience it you will want to show your partner what to do. You'll find some suggestions on how in Chapter 9.

The Sensual Mind: Fantasy

Our imaginations are a very powerful tool for exploring erotic ideas. You can have a wonderful "playtime" by learning how to fantasize, and can build sexual energy for your next pleasuring session, either by yourself or with a partner. There is nothing bad about having sexual thoughts.

Some people have trouble fantasizing, period. In fact, being able to visualize most anything is something of a skill that can be practiced. So if you are someone that draws a blank when you ask your mind to come up with a sexy scene, don't despair. You can learn how to fantasize.

How to Fantasize

Read these instructions, and then follow them. You'll start with what is familiar to you, and then go on to try erotic fantasies.

Sit or recline someplace quiet and comfortable. Lightly close your eyes, and pay attention to your breath. You don't have to do anything special to relax. Just noticing your breath going in and out, along with the rise and fall of your diaphragm, will help you to relax.

Close your eyes and picture a beautiful place that

you've been before. If all you see is "mud," then try to picture an easy part of the scene, like the blue sky or a tree. Let the details come out of the mud, like stars popping out in the night sky. Enjoy your beautiful scene for a few minutes.

See if you can put action into the scene. The action can be simple, such as seeing yourself walking in the scene, or touching something like sand, grass, or leaves that appear. You can either view your scene as if you were looking at it through your eyes, or watch your figure in the scene as if you were standing outside of yourself.

Now create a story that occurs in the scene. Again, it can be simple, such as taking out a picnic lunch and enjoying it by your self or with a partner.

Repeat this for several days. If you still have a hard time visualizing, then find a book of artwork or photos and practice by looking at the image, then closing your eyes and recreating it. You can do this over and over again with the same image to wake up your brain and begin to see things in your imagination more vividly. Then try seeing your own beautiful place in your mind's eye.

Once you can successful create an imaginary nonsexual scene, try using erotic imagery. An easy erotic scene might be to see yourself being undressed by your partner or someone else you find attractive. Notice how your breathing changes or if you become aroused. Let yourself play with the scene. You can be with your partner in as gentle or aggressive way as you wish.

What if you're unsure if your fantasies are normal? Be assured that most every fantasy that you might have would be considered okay. Just because an older man suddenly envisions a 17-year-old girl doesn't mean he is a sex offender.

However, fantasies can be disturbing. For example, if the same older man fantasized about young children and then found himself thinking of ways to meet young children in reality, then there would be concern that the fantasies were disturbing.

In the same way, a woman might fantasize about being raped (which is, interestingly, quite common) but not actually wish to experience rape. But if she started putting herself in harm's way, for example, getting very drunk at parties where she didn't really know anyone, then the fantasies may become troubling.

If you have a fantasy that you're not sure about, the best thing is not to overreact or beat yourself up. If the fantasy reappears, or if you can only have orgasm when you have the same upsetting fantasy, you can try to "morph" or change the fantasy yourself. If you continue to have problems, though, do seek assistance from a sex therapist.

Surprisingly, Good Sex Starts with Your Breath

As I stated earlier, the secret of good lovemaking is to be both aroused and relaxed. Getting aroused is natural. Getting so aroused that you get lost in the act and forget your partner, or have an orgasm before you wish, is not so great. (Though you should be gentle with yourself is this has been your experience.) Some people have the opposite problem--they have difficult getting aroused because they can never relax.

So you want to learn to breathe. I know, you're thinking, *this is crazy, I'm breathing right now!* But I want you to breathe with a purpose, which is to be able to cool yourself down if you get too hot, or relax enough so you can heat yourself up if you're too cool.

There are all kinds of ways to learn deep breathing, but over time I have found this is what works.

Do this daily, outside the bedroom. Practice when you are both stressed and relaxed. Remind yourself to breathe by putting a little colored sticky dot someplace where you will routinely see it, like on the phone or dashboard. Then breathe whenever you are on the phone or when the car is stopped at a light.

Sit with feet on the floor, legs uncrossed. Put your hands loosely on your thighs. Take a few normal breaths. Notice if your breath "catches" anywhere; that's a sign that you are tense and need to relax.

Bring your palms to the sides of your torso so that they are on the lowest ribs. Breathe in. You should feel your lowest ribs move out. Breathe out. You should feel your lowest ribs move back to their starting position.

Usually, you breathe in through the nose and out through the mouth, but don't get too hung up on any of this. The last thing you want to do is try to perfect your breath. Talk about making yourself nuts! You are just trying to learn to harness your breath as a tool for focusing yourself and distracting yourself from anxiety.

By practicing outside the bedroom, you will be able to use deep breathing on cue while you are making love.

How do you do this without disrupting the whole shebang? Read on.

Chapter 8

8. Foreplay: The Heart of Passionate Sex

Foreplay isn't just the way in which you touch your partner. Foreplay is also a state of mind. Foreplay is a time when you can let go of everything else that is on your mind and focus entirely on pleasure. Foreplay *is* play, adult play. It is a way to connect with your partner on the most intimate level. And, it gives you a chance to explore your sexuality.

Foreplay does a lot of different things that can help the two of you have better sex:

- You can use foreplay to relax before you go on to have orgasm in whatever way pleases you.

- Foreplay helps you bond with your partner through loving touch, kisses, and looking into one another's eyes.

- The body is prepared for orgasm through foreplay. The genitals become tingly and engorged when the senses and erogenous zones of the body are stimulated.

- You can experiment with all kinds of sensations and fantasy during foreplay. You can try different moods, different types of touch, different materials, different music, and so on. You can keep things varied so that you can enjoy sex together for years.

Not only that, but foreplay creates the good kind of tension—the buildup of physical, mental, and emotional energy that prepares the body for the wonderful release that you experience from orgasm.

Angie's Story

I was married once before, in my early twenties, to a man that I thought was a pretty good lover but who couldn't be faithful. After we divorced, I experimented sexually with quite a few partners. At least, that's what I called experimentation—just being with a new man and experiencing a new sexual "high".

Then I met and married Eric. We had a great sex life for the first two years, but then things started to get stale, and rather quickly, too. It was confusing for both of us. I even questioned if we were really supposed to be together. Finally, one of us—I don't remember who— broke the ice and started the conversation going.

What we discovered is that once the early fireworks have stopped, we have to create our own. For both of us, it was being in tune with our own sexual needs and being able to communicate that. We also had to be open to trying new things.

So, for me, it meant being the passive partner sometimes and letting Eric love me up. I learned that I could really enjoy relaxing and receiving pleasure. Plus, it's a big turn-on for Eric to see me respond to what he is doing.

For Eric, it meant accepting that I needed to use a toy like a vibrator to get aroused before we had intercourse so that I could have an orgasm, and not seeing himself as less than a man. Eric also learned how to tell me to what he wanted from oral sex, like if he needed me to sit in a certain position while he watched.

The most important thing we learned, I think, is that to be passionate lovers we really needed to communicate. We couldn't just expect chemistry to do it all if we wanted to have a good sex life. And, we couldn't just read each other's minds, either.

Everyone's sexuality is unique to them. Think of it as something like a personality. Just as you have preferences about food, colors, and movies, you have sexual preferences, too. And the way you view and approach the world is also reflected in your sexuality.

Whether you approach life with joy and a sense of freedom or are one of those people who take time to warm up to new things, you will likely approach sex in the same way.

(There are exceptions, though. We all know the stereotype of Marion the librarian, the introvert who wears her thick, sensual hair in a bun and covers up her secret with a dumpy tweed suit, or Casper Milquetoast who is completely uninhibited in bed. When it comes to sex, you never can tell, and that's one of the mysteries that make it fun!)

Which means that there is no right or wrong way to make love. That's why learning a list of sex techniques or positions can be helpful, but for the long haul you need good basic knowledge, an attitude of curiosity, and an unselfish motivation for the best sex.

Passionate Sex Requires Intimacy

If you are going to enjoy the kind of sex that you crave, you need to have intimacy. Intimacy means being able to be able to talk about your sexual preferences without judgment from your partner.

Even if your partner isn't interested in the same kind of sex you prefer, being able to tell your partner about it can help the two of you work out a compromise. For example, if your partner likes oral sex, but you don't, maybe you can agree that you are going to learn how to give the best manual sex your partner could ever experience. Or maybe you can give in once a month in exchange for a massage that your partner frankly finds kind of boring to do.

But intimate sex does more for a couple than just allowing them to experience a more satisfying bedroom relationship. When you allow yourself to relax and be fully yourself during lovemaking, you create a special bond between yourself and your partner.

You also lessen the natural tension that exists between two people living under the same roof together. Something about holding someone in your arms and looking in their eyes during sex makes it easier to understand that your partner is human, too—a spirit who needs love and caring, just like you do.

You don't have to tell your partner everything about your sexuality all at once. In fact, you may not know what to say! That's all right, you can learn as you go. And you can let your partner find out more about you over time as you gain trust and experience in talking about sex.

Ready to learn more? Read on for secrets of foreplay.

But What If I Don't Like Foreplay?

We're not talking about lima beans and salt cod here. We're talking about a natural function of the body. "I don't like foreplay" is like saying, "I don't like to shower," or, "I don't like to eat."

All that being said, I do understand. Foreplay can be, well, embarrassing. You have to take off your clothes and move in ways that feel awkward. You may feel like you're on stage giving a performance. You may wonder what your partner is thinking about you. You may feel guilty for having fun when you don't feel worthwhile.

Does this describe someone like you? If so, did you skip past the first part of this book? Perhaps you need to go back, read, and reflect. Try to learn what is holding you back from just letting go and enjoying something that is natural, relaxing, and good for you and your relationship?

Or maybe you just need to figure out how it all goes together. How do you engage the senses, pay attention to your partner, and still enjoy yourself without worrying?

Let's start with one of the major delights of foreplay: to give and receive pleasurable feelings through the senses, especially the sense of touch.

That's basic, yes, but it's something that gets missed when people are making love. People think good foreplay is all about being able to stand or lie in a certain position while still licking all the important parts. It isn't. Once again, it's about giving and receiving pleasure through the senses, especially through the sensitive nerves of the hands and skin.

Preparing for Sensual Foreplay

One of the ways that couples ruin passion for one another is by not building "bridges" to intimate activity in the bedroom:

Claudia: *Ian's approach to lovemaking was to roll over just after we turned out the lights and announce, "I'm horny." Gee, what a way to get a girl hot, eh?*

Bruce: *My wife would let me know she wanted sex by running her toenails up and down my calf. I mean, I was glad she initiated, but it kind of grossed me out!*

Nancy: *I really feel sexy when my husband and I have had a great conversation over a glass of wine, but does he listen when I tell him that? No! All he does is pinch my butt as we're going upstairs to bed to let me know he wants sex.*

Pretty lame stuff, right? Yet you can be sure it's happening between couples all over the globe.

I think most of these people would say the same thing: They wouldn't mind a little jab in the calf or pinch on the butt if their partner showed an effort at least some of the time that he or she understood making love was a time of emotional as well as physical intimacy and release.

Learning about Touch

Couples let each other know in all kinds of ways that they are thinking about having sex, but touch is probably one of the loveliest ways to get each other warmed up. Listed below are four common types of touch. You can start anywhere on this "scale" and work your way up. Always listen to your partner if he or she says she wants to stop at a certain place.

Comforting touch: When you put your arm around your partner or rub your partner's arm to help him or her feel better, you are using comforting touch.

People frequently need comforting touch and don't even realize it. Hence, they don't ask for it. However, they often know that they don't experience it often enough, because if their partner approaches them for sex without ever offering comforting touch, they may express hurt or anger. Comforting touch is an important part of any passionate relationship.

Loving touch: The purpose of this type of touch is not just to give support, but also to express a feeling. Loving touch is more intimate. Holding hands, giving a massage as a prelude to lovemaking, stroking your partner's hair, or even light kisses are all part of loving touch.

Much of the same ideas about the need for loving touch are explained above. Couples that want to experience passionate sex will express affection with loving touch, knowing that it may or may not lead to sex.

Erotic touch: Erotic touch is more intense and intimate. Strokes are longer, hands may press more tightly, and the erogenous zones—the parts of the body that feel good and make you feel aroused—are explored.

Erotic touch is often a prelude to great, passionate sex. In fact, it is nearly impossible to have passionate sex without this loving, sensual type of touch.

Sexual touch: Sexual touch is directly touching the erogenous zones. Sexual touch without comforting, loving, or erotic touch beforehand is often unwelcome. That is why most women, for example, don't like their partner to come up behind them while they are folding laundry or doing dishes to squeeze their breasts. It may feel good to do it, but it frequently doesn't feel good to be on the receiving end. (The next time you have an urge to squeeze, try some loving touch first and see if you don't get a different reaction.)

It's important that both partners understand these types of touch. That way, not only can you use this knowledge to build trust, affection, and passion, but you can also communicate with one another about what type of touch you would like to give or receive. For many couples, just knowing about different types of touch can bring a whole new level of understanding and intimacy into their relationship.

The Bedroom Environment

I wish you could see the looks on people's faces when I ask them what their bedroom is like. They usually look at one another right away, not in anger, but in recognition that maybe there's something not too sexy about the room where they usually make love.

Keep the bedroom a place for two activities: making love, and sleeping. It's best not to even have a TV in the bedroom, because it makes it all too easy to get absorbed in a program instead of your partner. Sometimes, though, a TV can be used for erotic viewing.

If that's your wish, at least store the TV in a cabinet that can be closed, or put a scarf over it when it is not in use. Turn off the telephone and cell phone, too. There can be no bigger drag than having the phone ring at the height of ecstasy.

Privacy

Everyone should have a lock on the bedroom door. Parents sometimes worry that their children will be frightened or that they won't be able to hear them if the door is closed. Believe me, if your child wants your attention that badly, he or she will figure out a way to get it! Better to have a lock on the door so that you can feel safe and comfortable about making love.

You also may want to think about blocking the sounds of lovemaking from floating out of your room. Use heavy drapes and rugs if such sounds are an issue. You can also have extra insulation put into the walls between bedrooms if you want to ensure privacy.

Decorating Your Bedroom

Whether you like feeling like you're in a quaint French bed and breakfast or a zippy modern scene, the most important thing is that you have a way of storing clutter. Put away clothing and shoes, hang up bath towels, and keep only essential items on your nightstand.

In general, cool colors like blues, greens, and grey

are calming, while warm colors like reds and oranges excite the senses. Most people enjoy restful colors in the bedroom, but if you like hot pink and saffron yellow, go for it.

Lighting is also important. I don't recommend making love in the dark. Even if you are very self-conscious about your body, you would be better off keeping on a bit of clothing but still able to see your partner while making love. Looking into your lover's eyes and seeing your hands on each other can be quite arousing, plus it increases a sense of safety and intimacy.

Instead of keeping on some clothing, however, you could experiment with soft lighting from candles or low wattage or pink-tinted bulbs. While you are learning to become more skilled as a lover (or masseuse) you might want to have more light so that you can see what you are doing, but if you need to start with a little illumination and gradually increase the amount of light, that's okay, too.

You may also want to have a piece of artwork that expresses love. A wooden Indonesian sculpture of lovers in an embrace or a poster of Gustav Klimt's "The Kiss" can remind you that the bedroom is a great place for sex.

A live plant or a vase of flowers can add grace and energy to your lovemaking environment. Try a peace plant, which cleanses the air of pollutants. Or, use silk plants or flowers; research shows that the mind sees beauty whether the plants are real or artificial.

Temperature

Give some thought to how warm or cold it is in the room. If you don't want to heat or cool the whole house to a temperature that is comfortable for you to be nude in your bedroom, just use a portable fan or air conditioning unit or small heater to keep the bedroom comfortable.

Pleasure Chest

Have a lockable cabinet that contains all of your toys, lubricants, erotic materials, etc. in your bedroom. That will keep your items safe from children or anyone else that enters your bedroom.

How to Start Foreplay

Even if you've been sexually active for a long time, you probably were never taught how to really make love to someone else. If you learned from a book of still photographs, from watching Hollywood movies, or, perhaps worst of all, from watching pornography, you may think you learned something, but you probably didn't.

Also, from the sad but true department, if your partner isn't very interested in sex, it is possible that you've missed the boat when it comes to lovemaking. You'd be surprised at how many men and women tell me privately that their beloved is just not very good in bed.

So this is how to be passionate in bed. But this isn't a formula, not a recipe. I'm giving you some basic ingredients, and it's up to you to put them together in a way that feels good, feels loving, and feels passionate. When you find the ways that these basic units fit together for you and your partner, you'll find yourselves building a whole rhythm to your lovemaking.

Being In the Moment

If you are old enough, you may recall a book that seemed to be everywhere called *Flow: The Psychology of Optimal Experience.* Written by Mihály Csíkszentmihályi, *Flow* tells readers that the way to a feeling of satisfaction and even happiness is to immerse yourself in whatever experience you are in, whether it's playing music or baking a cake.

Or even, dare I say it, making love.

What happens if you stop to think, stop to check in with yourself before every move you make?

You stop the flow. And in the process, sometimes foil your chance for pleasure that could be so much more fulfilling than what you currently have.

Of course, the difference with playing music or baking a cake is that these can be solitary experiences, with no distractions.

So don't distract one another when you are making love. Keep your attention on what is happening in your body, your heart, and your mind and express that to your lover. Let your experience unfold moment by moment without judgment.

Feeling Safe

Maybe you feel safe during lovemaking, but what about your partner? If your partner is timid or inhibited, creating a sense of safety in the bedroom might be a very important step as you intensify your lovemaking.

As you learn to make love in a new way, you may feel some uncomfortable emotions. Embarrassment, vulnerability, shame may easily come to mind, but even positive emotions like love and intimacy can be tough to tolerate. And in any case, we all know that change is often difficult.

The mixture of change, increased intimacy, and vulnerability can, well, really mess with your head. So acknowledge this with your partner and make an agreement as follows:

When one of us feels overwhelmed or nervous, we can signal each other that we need to feel safe. To do this, we will take a position of safety and either stay that way until we feel confident enough to go on or let our partner kindly know that we've had enough of a lovemaking session for the time being.

What kinds of signals can you use?

- A gentle shoulder tap.

- A "time out 'T'" with your hands.

- A few words, "I need to feel safe," or "I need to stop for a moment"

And what position might you take?

- Try lying on your sides while you hold hands and look at each other.

- Or get into "spoon" position if you are a more comfortable not looking directly at your partner.

- Or one of you can lie back and the other can lie on that person's chest.

- Sometimes, just maintaining a gentle touch is enough.

There's no right answer here. The important thing is to figure this out ahead of time so that you can just move into safety as needed without breaking the intimate connection you've tried to create. Much better than doing what some people do, which is getting up and dressing or running into the bathroom, no?

One more note: Please use this time to breathe! After awhile you may just be able to use your breath to feel safe and not have to stop at all.

Sensual Explorations for Two

Earlier in this book, you read about sensual self-exploration. Now you are about to read some ways to use your senses during foreplay. There are many ways to create sensual experiences in the bedroom. The more senses you engage, the more delightful sex can be. Here are some simple ways to heighten your pleasure.

Bathing. Try bathing or showering together before you have sex. Use glycerin soap in either an invigorating (birch, mint, sandalwood) or calming (lavender, vanilla) fragrance that you can both enjoy. This is a very delicious way to start a love making session and prepares you for oral sex if that's what you wish to do.

Sensuous Snacks. You can start with a tray of fruits and bits of chocolate to feed one another. Or keep a split of champagne ready to enjoy during your lovemaking session. If you don't want to use alcohol, fruit nectar or sparkling water makes a nice, refreshing substitute.

Fragrance. You can simply dab some aromatherapy oil on a cotton ball and put it into a ceramic tray to bring some scent into the room. Fragrant candles or incense are another suggestion. No reason you couldn't have some fresh flowers nearby, as well. And if your bedroom window overlooks a fragrant garden, why not open the windows?

Textures. You can have a lot of fun playing around with different fabrics. Try chiffon or silk scarves, large and small feathers, terry cloth or velvet mitts, or almost anything you can think of to run across your partner's body. Try different locations and different levels of pressure to see what you and your partner enjoy.

Your voice. Say sexy things to your partner. Compliment face and hands as well as sexy body parts. Tell your partner what you are going to do, and encourage your partner to tell you the same.

Your tongue and breath. Blow your warm breath over your partner's body, wherever you think it will delight. Use your tongue in little or long sensual licks, all over. Try doing the same thing with an ice cube or chip in your mouth.

Your body. Use a different body part to stroke your partner's body. If you are a woman, run your breasts all over your partner. If you are a man, touch your partner playfully with your penis. Use your feet.

Use your behind. Have fun.

Body-to-body.   If you are a woman, you are presumably the smaller, lighter partner, but if not, just reverse the instructions for this activity.

Have your partner lay back, legs slightly splayed. You then lie on top of your partner, making yourself comfortable so that you can place your head on his shoulder. Relax. If your partner gets an erection, just enjoy that it's there, but neither of you need to do anything about it. Simply enjoy the feeling of skin on skin. Maybe add some massage oil. Soak in the pleasure of being held and lightly caressed with nothing to do and nowhere to go.

Chapter 9

9. Hands are Wonderful Sex Toys

It would be almost irresponsible not to mention the pleasures of manual sex.

So you need to stay just as in tune with your partner's responses during manual sex as you do during intercourse. If you get distracted or show as much interest in manual sex as you do scrubbing out the sink, it will show and your partner may be hurt.

Are You Ready?

Remember at the beginning of the book I talked about sex in the 21st century? How enlightened we are all supposed to be? Well, if you want proof that it isn't so, think for a minute about attitudes toward manual sex, aka masturbation.

Myths about masturbation persist into the present day. While no one believes that masturbation will make hair grow on your palms (truly, there was a physician who published such stuff way back in the old days), many believe that masturbation is a last ditch activity, and still "not nice," "dirty," or even "gross".

A few very conservative religions prohibit masturbation, but many do not. Masturbation is considered to be a healthy activity. Through self-pleasure, you can learn about your body--what it feels like as you get excited, how tension builds, and what you like done to your body to help release that tension. If you haven't yet read Chapter 9 on manual pleasure, then please do.

There are some inspiring reasons to use hands and fingers to make your partner feel good and to bring them to orgasm. Your hands and fingertips have incredible sensitivity, as do a man's penis and a woman's clitoris. It's a pretty awesome match.

And then there's the fatigue factor. Sometimes having intercourse really does take more energy than one or both partners have for each other. Or sometimes one partner feels a need for physical release, and the other just isn't in the same place physically or mentally.

Part of the art of sex by hand is in the way you communicate to your partner what feels good. I may be contradicting myself here, but when it comes to handling your partner's privates, what feels good to you may not feel good to your partner.

Once you know what feels good to you, you can show your partner--if you are ready. If it is embarrassing for you to masturbate alone, then masturbating in front of a partner might seem very awkward.

It can be very helpful, then, to understand your

own body so that at the very least you can tell your partner what you like and don't like when it comes to manual sex.

One thing is certain: Neither partner should force the other to masturbate in front of the other, even for "educational" purposes.

If one of you is comfortable both talking about masturbation and masturbating in front of your partner, and the other isn't, then start a gentle discussion. You could ask if you partner has ever liked to self-pleasure, or what they think about it. Share your own attitudes.

If your partner is open to mutual masturbation, it can still be awkward to get things started. You could make an agreement to take turns showing each other how you masturbate. Decide whether or not you want to climax during your "demonstration," or if you want to have an orgasm in another way as part of a lovemaking session.

Show 'n' Tell

A delightful way to learn about each other's bodies is to show your partner explicitly how you like to be touched. This activity is best done nude, but you can also do it lightly clothed if you are more comfortable that way.

Take turns, with each of you spending about 10-15 minutes exploring the other's body. The receiving partner should recline, propped up with pillows so you can reach beyond your torso to your own genitals and legs. The giving partner should sit comfortable to the receiver's side.

If you are the giver, ask your partner if he or she would like you to apply talc, lotion or almond oil to you as you guide his or her hands over your body. If so, warm the lotion or oil in your palms first.

Keep your hands and wrists relaxed as you permit your partner to lightly place your hands on his or her body. Let your hands settle a moment; both of you can take a deep relaxing breath.

As the recipient, you can glide your partner's hands over your body in a way that feels good to you. You can keep one of your partner's hands still over one part of your body, while you move your partner's hand to another. Or you can glide them up and down your body at the same time.

Move your partner's hands at a pace that feels good to you. If you want more pressure, put more pressure on your partner's hands. If you want very little pressure, then keep your hands very lightly on your partner's.

When you've reached the end of your agreed-upon time period, or when you feel you'd like your partner to stop touching you, pause and thank your partner before you switch roles.

If you'd like, you can use this activity as a type of foreplay, or you can agree that it would be just wonderful to stop and save lovemaking for another time, whatever feels right to you.

If You're a Woman Giving a Man Manual Sex...

Some women are very confused about manual sex, aka the "hand job." Men complain that their partners never touch their penis, or when they do they either hold it as if it is dainty, or grab it like it's a martini shaker. The penis is neither. It's a remarkably sensitive, responsive organ that men just love to have touched!

Your partner most likely will enjoy a firm touch, but how firm will depend on him. If he doesn't tell you, ask. Be sure to use lubricant; although it makes the penis slippery, it will allow you to have both a good grip and create the friction your partner enjoys.

If you don't have any lubricant available, you can use saliva, but it will dry out quickly. Without suitable lubricant, you will probably grip less firmly, while still keeping up a steady, stroking rhythm up and down the shaft of your lover's penis.

When giving a hand job, you can either lie down by your partner's side and reach down to touch his penis, or you can sit by his side or between his legs. You could also have him sit on the edge of the bed or a chair while you kneel in front of him; he could be standing, facing you while you kneel; or you could be behind him as he sits, reaching around to the front.

If you need inspiration, here are some ideas:

You can hold your partner's penis at the base, with your thumb and forefinger positioned so that they are closest to the head. Keep your grip rather loose as you glide your hand up the shaft. Use more pressure with your thumb and forefinger as you near the head of the penis (how much depends on your partner). Stop just short of the tip, and then fluidly glide your hand back down the shaft. Start slowly and gradually go faster. You can add pleasure by twisting your grip a little bit one way as you go up, and twisting a bit the other way as you go down the shaft.

Another way to go is to turn your grip the other way, so that your thumb and forefinger are closest to the base. Bring your hand up the shaft, rub the palm of your hand over the head, and then bring your hand back down the shaft so that it ends up in the starting position.

Try lacing your fingers together on one side of your partner's penis and locking your thumbs together on the other, creating a kind of tube. Now, using a firm grip, move your hands up and down the shaft. You can use a lightly pulsing motion with your hands as they travel.

If your partner's penis is not especially hard, you can use wrap one hand around the shaft, bring it up to the head, and then do the same with your other hand. Keep up this hand-over-hand motion until your partner becomes erect, or continue until he ejaculates.

Do you continue until your partner ejaculates? And if so, what do you do? That depends on your partner. Some men like to have a woman continue stroking quickly to orgasm, some men like to have the speed of the stroking slow down, some like to be stroked in time with their ejaculation. You and your partner can experiment, or your partner can let you know what he wants.

It's also perfectly normal for him to want to finish himself off, so don't be hurt or put out if he does so. He may also prefer to have an orgasm inside of you, but if you are not ready, say so. Contrary to popular belief, he is not going to explode if you don't have intercourse right away. Ask for what you want or need to get ready for intercourse, all the while continuing to stimulate your partner.

If You're a Man Giving a Woman Manual Sex...

While most men can probably figure out how to find the clitoris (see diagram on page 78), learning how to manually stimulate a woman can be a little trickier. Women vary greatly in terms of sensitivity. Also, some women may not be accustomed to touching themselves and may have a difficult time telling you what feels good. Best to start slow and take your time to explore.

The best position is to lie by your partner's side so that you have access to her genitals. Begin by simply letting your hand rest on her mons and vulva, allowing your partner to get used to being touched. (Remember, while you may handle your penis all the time, unless a woman masturbates she may not touch her genitals much except to clean them.)

Once you know your partner is comfortable with your hand on her genitals, begin to gently move your entire hand, either around or up and down.

Next, use your fingertips to touch the labia majora, or outer lips. Try using one fingertip to trace one side of the lip from perineum to the mons, then down the other side. Or gently pinch the outer and inner lips between thumb and index finger, touching your way up and down between perineum to clitoris.

You can also try using your index and ring finger to separate the labia while you use the middle finger to stroke between them.

As for actually touching the clitoris, most women prefer it to be touched through the hood, or covering. Lubricant can be helpful, too, letting your fingers slip over and around the hood. You can use a single digit, usually your index finger, to circle the hood around the clitoris.

You can also try rolling the clitoris through the hood by rubbing the hood between your thumb and index finger. Your partner might also like "vibration unplugged": Put one, two, three, or four fingers over the hood and surrounding area and vibrate your hand rapidly. You can move your hand back and fort, around, or up and down. Just keep your fingers pressed gently while you make this vibrating contact.

The clitoris isn't the only area that women like stimulated. The first two inches or so of the vagina also contain nerve endings, so try inserting a finger or two and using them like a small dildo, drawing them in and out. You can then put your thumb on the clitoris and stimulate both areas at once.

The renowned G-spot is a bit of a mystery because not all women have one, and not all women that do like G-spot stimulation. But some women say that the G-spot is the most sensitive area of all, so you might want to try exploring it. Just don't take it personally if it doesn't, well, hit the spot. Above all, be respectful of this area, which is considered to be perhaps the most intimate place you can touch on a woman's body.

The G-spot is an area about 1-1/2 to 2 inches deep into the vagina. The best way to find it is to have the woman lie on her back. You can sit by her side at about hip level, or sit between her legs. Insert a lubricated index finger in her vagina about where you would guess the location is, and use a "come hither" motion on the top side to stimulate the spot. Besides knowing about how deep the G-spot is inside the vagina, you may be able to feel where the G-spot is because the texture of the G-spot may be different than the rest of the vagina.

Of course, your partner's response is the best indicator of all. If she tells you to stop, do so right then, because unwanted G-spot stimulation is very uncomfortable.

On the other hand, she may feel something, but not be sure of the sensation. Continue to explore, checking in to see if this is comfortable or uncomfortable for your partner. Or you might "hit the spot" and your partner may find herself having an orgasm.

One more thing to note: Sometimes women have a strong emotional reaction to a G-spot orgasm. It isn't clear exactly why, but this is a very deep, private place in a woman's body. So don't be shocked if you get some tears, just add some comforting or loving touch and see what is needed in the moment to make the woman feel good again.

Chapter 10

10. Oral Pleasure

Lovers sometimes have strong preferences regarding oral pleasure, both giving and receiving. Just as with masturbation, oral sex is saddled with myths about things like vaginal odor, having to swallow semen, gagging, or being put into a submissive position as giver.

None of these myths need to color your own perception of oral pleasure. Approach oral sex with an open mind and experience it for yourself. With a bit of knowledge and preparation, you may find that giving and receiving oral sex may open up a new vista of pleasure to explore.

Oral Sex: Man to Woman

If you are the woman and are new to receiving oral sex, you may be nervous about having your partner so up close and personal with your genitals.

Whatever shape, size, or color your genitals, they will be attractive to your partner. If you love and enjoy your own genitals, your partner will find that exciting, too.

If you have never done so, you really need to look at your genitals using good lighting and a hand mirror.

Admire your vulva; notice the vestibule, or opening to the vagina; examine the delicate structure of your clitoris.

Now when your lover wishes to gift you with oral sex, remind yourself of the beauty that he sees when he goes down on you.

A word about odor. The vagina is a remarkable organ that maintains a certain ph balance. The vagina sloughs off its walls, just as your skin does, to get rid of old cells in its lining. Maintaining cleanliness is important, but so is maintaining a healthy ph balance.

One way to wash your genitals is with a mild soap, such as a baby soap for sensitive skin, and to rinse your genitals thoroughly with warm--not hot--water. You can also simply rinse your genitals without using soap-- though in our clean-driven culture, you will probably feel uncomfortable without lathering up at least a little.

Just before having oral sex, you could also use a baby wipe and follow it with a quick clear water rinse.

It is impossible to get rid of ALL odor. Your genitals are sex organs and meant to have a bit of odor. There are pheromones, oils, and hormones in that area of your body. To be absent of odor would be very odd. So accept your unique sweet musky smell and appreciate it as a sign of womanly passion.

Now all you need to do is relax...aaaaah!

And while it's generally nice to shave if you know you're going to make love, it's actually almost de rigueur if you are going to give oral sex. A smooth face feels much better against delicate tissues.

Also consider your position. You can have your lover sit on the edge of the bed so that you can kneel and pleasure her. You can have her lie back on the bed, and you can position yourself so that you are lying on your torso. Or you can have your lover start by kneeling above your head, then bringing her genitals to your lips.

Another way is to lie at a right angle to your lover's hips and come in to pleasure her from the side. Try different positions and angles until you find one you both like.

Best to start by kissing, nibbling, and licking your partner's inner thighs. In fact, you can start at the feet or ankles and work your way up slowly. When you arrive at the folds of the vulva, gently use the tip of your tongue to tickle and nudge the flesh.

Whatever you do, don't hone it right on her clitoris. Remember, it is *very* sensitive, and you need to approach it with tender loving care. Most women prefer a slow, gentle approach, so start by kissing and caressing her body everywhere.

Some women will prefer that you start with kisses on the lips, working your way down to her breasts, abdomen, and then genitals. Others love to have feet, ankles, and thighs caressed along the way. And others, of course, enjoy all of it, so just try different things to find explore preferences.

Now for the fun part: stimulating her genitals with your tongue and lips. In general, firm strokes of your tongue are better than little flicks and jabs, but you never know. Just pay attention to your lover's responses; if she winces, make a note that what you just did isn't a preference, and try something else. Listen for your partner's moans and observe the way she moves her body.

Lick up and down, side to side, and all around the vulva and the clitoris. You can also put your tongue into the vagina every now and then. Fingers can also pleasure your lover's vagina as you lick. Again, notice what makes your partner swoon with pleasure and keep doing it.

Your lover may or may not have an orgasm with oral sex, especially if you are newly experimenting. She may be a little shy that you are so "up close and personal" with her privates, or she may not be sure about what she is feeling. You can always check in and ask if she'd like you to continue, or if she'd like some other kind of sex play.

And of course, you can also ask for your turn...

Note on male cleanliness: A man's genitals can

also have an odor to them, which your lover may or may not appreciate. Similar oils and hormones that fragrance a woman's vulva and surrounding areas also fragrance you. So you may also want to wash before receiving oral sex, or use a baby wipe followed by a water rinse.

If you are a woman giving oral sex to a man, you can also consider position. If you are the right heights to do so comfortably, your partner may wish to stand while you kneel. He can also lie prone while you position yourself between his thighs, or you can lie to his side.

Begin by touching your partner all over. As your partner may do with your body, you may start at the lips, travel to the neck, kiss his chest and abdomen, and then work your way down to his penis. Or you may want to tease his feet, ankles, and thighs.

Once you've warmed your partner up, you may want to explore his penis, scrotum, and perineum (space between testicles and anus) with your hand. Remember that the head, or glans, of the penis is the most sensitive to touch. Most men also find the frenulum--the indentation where the glans meets the shaft--the most sensitive part of the head.

Your partner may or may not be erect when you choose to put his penis into your mouth. It's perfectly all right to take his penis into your mouth before he gets hard. You can use your hand and your mouth to bring him to an erection.

As you explore his erect penis with your mouth, keep your lips over your teeth to guard against scratching his fragile tissue. Keep your lips very moist, and slide them down the shaft as far is you find comfortable. It is unnecessary to go any further than that; just use your hand around the bottom portion of the shaft of his penis. No need to gag!

Try to keep your mouth and hand going up and down his penis in unison. In other words, when your lips go up, so does your hand, and vice versa. If your lips get tired, it's okay to stop for a few moments and use just your hand. Pull your hand up the shaft, then stroke around the head, then take your hand back down again. Go back to fellatio when you are ready.

Do you have to swallow? No! You can if you wish, but if you don't want to, then just let your partner know it isn't something you'd like to experience. It's just a matter of preference.

And what about the fear of gagging? Keeping your gag reflex in check requires two things. First, you have to know what you are doing in the physical sense, and then you have to be able to trick yourself a little in the mental sense.

Physically, you need to know that you only have to take as much of your partner's penis into your mouth as you are comfortable with. You don't have to be a "deep throat."

Try to position yourself so that your partner can see your attention to his penis and use your hands to caress the rest of the shaft and his scrotum and testicles; that will likely be more than enough stimulation.

You should also try inhaling through your nose as you move up your partner's shaft and exhaling as you move back down. You can certainly stop moving altogether if you are getting overwhelmed or find yourself gagging despite your best efforts. Just use your hands to pleasure your partner while you regroup and decide how you'd like to continue.

Mentally, you have to tell yourself to relax and not to gag! If you start thinking about the fact that you have a large item in your mouth, you may get anxious and gag. Just remember, your partner's penis isn't going to become detached and lodge in your throat, suffocating you. Let your partner know that you are practicing and not to get upset if you stop.

Also, let him know that he has to take care not to thrust or pump too much or you may actually gag. You can keep your hands on his groin to remind him to let you do the work, or you pause and gently remind him.

What you do need to do is keep up your stroking action with your hand when you sense your partner is about to ejaculate, or tell him to let you know, perhaps with a little tap on your shoulder, that he is about to have orgasm. He won't enjoy it if you simply pull away like a geyser is about to blow. Keep up your loving caresses until he is finished, so that if you don't keep him in your mouth until the end he really won't mind.

A word about flavored lubricants: Yes, flavored lubricants can help make oral sex more fun for some people. Try to find lubricants that use natural flavors and are sugar-free, as sugar is a natural environment for the growth of yeast. And if you're going to use chocolate sauce, honey, or syrup, for goodness' sake, shower quickly so that you don't invite an infection.

Try these sexy tips for giving better oral sex:

- Tie your hair back so that your partner can watch you making love to his penis.

- Or, if your hair is long enough, let it dangle down over his groin and testicles.

- Let your partner suck on one or two of your fingers while you suck on his penis.

- Give some attention to his scrotum and testicles.

- Tease the frenulum with some flicks and licks of your tongue now and then.

- When your partner is very excited, pick up the rhythm and create more suction with your mouth.

Hair Down There

A word about pubic hair: for women, it actually serves a purpose, providing a bit of padding during intercourse. However, it is perfectly fine for either sex to trim, shave, or wax as desired. (But, only if the owner of said pubic hair wishes it to be trimmed, shaved, or waxed!)

Chapter 11

11. Intercourse: Passionate Fusion

Intercourse.

It's held out like the Holy Grail of the human sexual experience.

I'm old enough to remember watching entire TV series that were focused, season after season, on whether or not the main characters were going to have sex. And how many movies have you watched where the couples decide to stimulate each other manually instead of proceeding to intercourse?

If there are other ways of getting sexual satisfaction, and if you are not trying to get pregnant, why bother with intercourse anyway?

Most people say that intercourse makes them feel connected to their partner. Coming together as one is as intimate as you can be with another person. Some people feel it is a sacred moment; others simply revel in the intensity of the experience.

Yet for some people, intercourse is disappointing or difficult. It can leave them feeling empty, used, or ashamed.

Intercourse Made Simple

You may or may not find intercourse the "be all, end all" of having sex with your partner, but there are definitely ways to make the experience good.

First of all, ditch the idea of simultaneous orgasms. (That's what it's called when people have orgasm at the same time.) Nice if they happen, but unnecessary--a parlor trick.

A lot of people think that simultaneous orgasm means that you are really in synch with each other. And that may be true. But you are two different people, not conjoined twins, so if you have different experiences during sex, that's okay.

I'm not saying not to bother experimenting to see if you can both have an orgasm at the same time, but I am saying not to make it a big goal or to get bent out of shape if it doesn't occur.

Second, stop expecting fireworks every time you have intercourse. Or, for that matter, any time you are sexually active together, whether it's with intercourse or manual or oral sex. Here's what's normal: Sometimes sex is amazing. Sometimes it is good. Sometimes it is okay. And sometimes, yes, it sucks.

But not usually.

Basically, it's just like any other experience. You

wouldn't expect every meal you eat to bowl you over, so why put so much pressure on sex?

But if you're a woman, don't just lie there. And if you're a man, don't just turn saw your penis into your partner's vagina.

What do you do instead? There are several common positions that you should experiment with. You can start in one and move to another. And don't worry about being clumsy; generally it's only in the movies that people can do the kinds of acrobats that let them cling together as one while they flip from one position to another.

As you get more used to being in different positions, you'll move a little more gracefully. But if you do end up rolling off the bed and onto the floor, just laugh and start over.

Sometimes people in my office (both men and women) complain of sex being "mechanical." None of the suggestions in this section are meant to be followed like a DYI manual. Spontaneity and expression are key to making love that feels good.

Too inhibited to be spontaneous in bed? Go back to the early sections of the book to figure out why. Talk to your partner or a therapist to figure out how to overcome your inhibitions.

Now, don't become unglued over the fact that you

have inhibitions. I can just imagine someone worrying themselves about their worries! Just accept that you have them, and start changing your attitudes and behaviors over time.

For example, if you are one to "just lie there" during intercourse, start moving. Maybe at first you will just move your hands a little more over your partner's body. Maybe you will just tilt your head back a bit when your partner does something particularly delicious.

You don't have to be a contortionist to demonstrate your enjoyment, but you can also try moving your legs, for example, bending your knees and clasping your partner between your thighs.

And if you're the male partner, how about relaxing and taking your time to enjoy the journey? You could stroke the hair away from your partner's forehead, or lean down and whisper something erotic in her ear.

If you feel vulnerable while you try being more expressive, that's normal. Making love does that to people--makes them feel a bit more open to another person. But allowing yourself to be vulnerable, to show your partner what you are feeling, not just physically but emotionally, perhaps even spiritually, and finding yourself not only accepted but cherished, is what builds trust over time.

One More Thing . . .

Always use lubricant! It upsets me to no end when I have a woman in my office or her partner complaining of vaginal dryness, and taking it as a personal sign that they are a failure as a lover. Women can lubricate more or less at different times of the month; even stress can affect how much vaginal lubrication there is.

Lubrication also changes with age, with many women becoming drier as they approach menopause. Therefore, vaginal lubricant makes a lousy measure of how great a lover a man is.

Besides, having intercourse can cause a little bit of wear and tear on a woman's tissues. So do yourselves a favor and just put lubricant on BOTH of you. And not just a little—a lot. Don't be stingy, lube is cheap. And use more if you are having a longer session of intercourse and it gets a little dry down there. (See the section on Toys and Accessories for info on different types of lube.)

Please note that having a little bit of soreness during or after intercourse is from little micro-tears and tiny abrasions caused by friction, not by lubricant.

Sex should never cause any more than that bit of soreness. If you feel terrible burning or pain, tell your gynecologist.

Sex Positions Everyone Can Love

Even though the ancient sex manual known as the *Kama Sutra* lists 64 positions, all you really need to know are the five basic positions, which can be varied according to your mood. The five basic positions are missionary, woman on top, side-by-side, rear entry, and standing.

Missionary Position

Better known as "vanilla sex," missionary position has gotten a bad rap for being boring. But sometimes it feels good to have the fronts of your torsos rubbing together, or having your lips close, or your hot breath on each other's faces.

One of the reasons the missionary position (woman on bottom, legs spread; man on top) is so popular is that it works well for making a baby. The man gets to thrust, which pretty much guarantees he will ejaculate. The woman being on the bottom allows the sperm to efficiently swim toward the cervix, where they'll enter and continue on their journey to fertilize the egg.

It isn't a bad position for pleasure, either, for some people. There are women who enjoy the feeling of being dominated by a man, or who like the feeling of the man's penis rubbing against her clitoris. Also, if she lifts her legs, she might enjoy deep thrusting and the feeling of the penis bumping up against her cervix.

Or she might not like any of this at all. She might feel like she has dead weight on top of her, she might prefer to have freedom of movement, she might like to touch her clitoris during intercourse, she might not feel her partner's penis on her clitoris, and she might dislike the feeling of her partner's penis bumping against her cervix.

Conversely, a man may or may not like being on top. He might like deep thrusting--or he might prefer a different angle. He might not like the fact that he cannot see his lover's body. He might not like the kind of stamina that is required for being on top.

To add a little pepper, try holding hands while you are in this position. If you are a woman, you can hold onto your partner's hips or buttocks and guide him the way that feels best to you. You can also put a pillow under your bottom so that your partner can penetrate you more deeply.

You could also try missionary position with the woman's legs on the *inside*, which can create more direct friction of the penis on the clitoris. Another variation is for the man to kneel between the woman's legs and lift her hips up onto him, so that his thighs become a sort of ramp. The advantage is that from this position he can watch penetration.

Or the man can try holding still and letting the woman bump and grind against him. Strong Kegel muscles can be quite nice for massaging the man's penis in this position.

The way in which you have intercourse is very much about preference. Don't get too hung up on the "right" way to have intercourse. Do what feels good. And to find out what feels good, try some of these other positions.

Woman on Top

This position is just what it's called--the woman sits astride her partner and lets his erect penis enter her vagina. The position has various advantages. First, it allows both partners to look at one another and to stroke one another's face, torso, and arms. Second, it allows a woman or her partner to more easily caress her clitoris and / or nipples for extra stimulation during intercourse.

Women can also experience extra stimulation against the clitoris by leaning forward or back while they slide up and down their partner's erect shaft.

And of course, this allows a couple to enjoy intercourse when a man is too tired to be on top.

If you are a woman, you may feel too self-conscious about your body to be on top. Until you feel freer, why not just wear a tank top or pretty bra? Then when you start to feel less inhibited, you can bare it all for dramatic effect.

If you are a man, you can bend your knees so that

your partner can lean back against you, or leave your legs flat, whatever you wish. You can prop yourself up with pillows, or sit up and nuzzle your partner's neck and breasts. You can stroke your partner's back when you sit up as well, and let yourself be caressed.

Rear Entry

This has the unfortunate distinction of sometimes being called "doggy style," which makes some people shy away from using this position. But remember the old cliché: Don't knock it 'til you've tried it.

In this position, the woman has her rear to her partner. She does not necessarily need to be on all fours, because if her partner is tall she will need to raise her buttocks. She can experiment by arranging her torso so that a pillow is tucked under her chest, or she may be most comfortable with her torso folded all the way down until her forehead touches the bed.

Like the other positions, this one has advantages as well. It allows deep thrusting if this is something that you both enjoy. If you are female you might find it exciting to feel your partner's testicles bump up against your clitoris as he thrusts in and out.

This is another position that allows a woman to easily stimulate her clitoris during intercourse. She can also use a vibrator on herself, and give her partner some extra tingles in the process.

The position also allows for some anal play, again if this is something both partners want to explore. Use lots of lube and go very slowly when you are first trying manual stimulation to a woman's anus. The anus has many nerve endings and many people, male and female, find anal play very erotic and exciting. (If it isn't your thing, and your partner wants to explore, see the section on Negotiating Sex.)

The big disadvantage is that you cannot see one another's facial expression or look into one another's eyes. Even if you don't object to the "animal" quality of this position, you might feel disconnected from your partner.

You can get around this by looking into a mirror, if one is available. Or you can agree that as soon as intercourse is finished you will spend some time stroking one another's faces and reconnecting. Again, see the section on Negotiating Sex for more ideas on how to compromise.

Scissors

This is a nice position to use when you are both a bit tired but still want to make love. The man lies on his side and the woman lies on her back, with her legs over his hips so that he can enter her. The position is called "scissors" because you will create a shape like an open pair of scissors.

The advantage is that it allows for somewhat

shallow penetration, which may be helpful for some women who become uncomfortable with deep thrusting at certain times of the month or who have some problem that makes sex painful at times. The woman can also self-pleasure her clitoris.

For a man, the shallow thrusting may help him maintain more control, since sensation is less intense.

The disadvantage of this position is that while you can look in your lover's eyes, your faces are too far from one another for kissing or caressing.

Woman in Lap (Lotus Position)

This is a popular tradition in tantric lovemaking because it allows very close contact. The man needs to sit up and cross his legs "Indian style." The woman then sits in his lap, positioning herself so that he can enter her. The man can hold the woman under her hips and she can stroke his neck and back. Slowly rock back and forth for a sensual experience.

An obvious advantage of this position is that the man can experience his partner's breasts pressed into his chest. Both partners can kiss each other's lips, neck, and ears.

On the Edge

In this position, the woman lies on her back with her butt near the edge of the bed. She lifts her legs so that the man can enter her while he stands at the edge of the bed. She can either bend her legs so that her knees are near her ears, or she can raise them perpendicular to her torso so that her feet are near her partner's ears.

This position has the advantage of allowing deep or shallow thrusting so there can be plenty of variation during intercourse. The woman can also caress her clitoris and nipples, as can her partner. If the man wishes, he can lean down and kiss his partner's lips and neck as well.

The disadvantage is that the woman is relatively passive in this position.

Variations on Variations

If you have looked at the *Kama Sutra*, the book of positions taken from tantric yoga, you'd certainly have to be an athlete in order to get into some of the pretzel bends displayed! And for others, you'd have to compliment one another in terms of size and strength. A man might have great difficulty having sex standing up if his partner is about the same size and weight.

So how can you mix it up without having a trapdoor in the ceiling that hides the trapeze? It isn't all that difficult.

You can use pillows and bolsters to prop yourselves up in any number of ways. A pillow under a woman's hips when she is on the bottom can help with deeper thrusting. A bolster under a man's knees and some pillows tucked around his neck and shoulders when he is on the bottom can make for a more comfortable ride.

Really, the point is get yourself uninhibited enough, secure enough, and adventurous enough to try whatever impulse you have.

Want to cup your partner's breasts? Want to run your nails down his or her back? Or give your partner a big, juicy kiss when you climax? Go for it!

If you are excited and show it, then that is exciting to your partner. And if your partner feels uninhibited, secure, and adventurous, then your partner may respond to you. That will excite you more, and soon things are escalating to what may become a peak experience of pleasure.

Chapter 12

12. After Play: When All is Said and Done

Here's a thought: Lovemaking is never over. The afterglow of sex should stay with you long after the orgasm and, if you've slumbered, long into the time before you make love again.

Once you've had a pleasuring session of any kind--affectionate cuddling, massage, or lovemaking--you should take a moment to acknowledge to each other how good being close has made you feel, or how relaxed, or how loved.

Whatever you do, when play and pleasure seem to have come to an end do not start with a critique. If something about the time you have spent together did not feel good or right to you, then hold that thought until you have a little distance. You have just spent some time together in which you have both been a bit vulnerable, let down your guard, and shared some intimacy.

This is not the time, then, to tell your lover that they need to brush their teeth, trim their nails, or to slow down or speed up. Just let things be. Unless your partner is zipping up their jeans and speeding off for a tour of duty, they'll be around long enough for you to gently say what is needed, and I'll discuss how in a moment.

No, now is the time for some gentle touch, some soothing words while you begin the process of becoming separate again. For a few minutes, for an hour, perhaps, you've been acting as one, as in synch with one another as you could be at that point in time.

Make this parting sweet. Whether you are falling asleep, taking a shower together, napping, or getting up to tend to what needs to be done, take a moment to share what felt good, to make eye contact, to kiss and to hug.

In the practice of Tantra, this is when you would thank your lover for a sacred encounter. When sex is treated as something wholly wonderful and special, then gratitude to your partner for allowing you to experience it is in order. Really, it doesn't matter whether you follow a spiritual practice at all. Giving your partner loving thanks is also a good idea.

This is not the time to mention that the ceiling needs painting or that the mechanic didn't fix that one rattle in the car. Nor should you jump up and check your Blackberry to see why it buzzed while you were having sex. (Next time, put the phone in another room of the house.)

If you are the male partner, you should politely check to see if your partner had an orgasm. Some women are shy about saying anything; checking in gives your partner an opportunity to let you know what happened.

If not, don't take it personally. Learning to have an orgasm can take a long time, as can just having orgasm itself. See if your partner would like you to stimulate her manually, or if she would like to do so herself while you cuddle and caress her body. Don't be offended if she tells you that she might like to use a toy. Better yet, suggest it yourself. She may need stronger stimulation or have more control in order to have an orgasm.

What do you talk about? Talk about your feelings for your partner. Tell your partner how much you love him or her. Or give your partner a compliment on their lovemaking technique. Let them know that you had shivers, goose bumps, or that your muscles have relaxed. Let your partner know how good it was to be together.

If you are going to fall asleep, let your partner know that you are drifting off so that they feel you care. If you are going to get up to shower, to wash your face, or whatever, give your partner a parting kiss before you jump up.

Is there cleanup that needs to be done? Help each other pick up the bottle of lubricant, any tissues or wipes, and clothing, if it matters in your household. Men: Always take care of your own condom if you use one!

Later, maybe the next morning or the next evening, whisper a sweet comment about your lovemaking into your lover's ear. Or touch them in a lingering way someplace that you touched during your pleasuring session, on an arm, leg, or cheek.

In this way you can still stay connected until the next time you make love. Then it won't be awkward or stressful to come together again, to be vulnerable once more, and to succumb to the pleasure of sex.

A quick note about quickies: Some couples enjoy them, others don't. Quickies work best if you are both already aroused for some reason, like you've just watched a hot movie or teased each other in some way. But sometimes just the thought of sneaking in a little action is fun. So do include the quickie as part of your sexual repertoire.

Chapter 13

13. All About Lubricants and Toys

Why Use Lube?

Lubricant does so much more than just make things wetter--though wet sex can be fun. Lubricant helps to moisten a woman's tender tissues. (A man's, too, if he wants to engage in anal play.) And while some people think that dry sex is better because it is tighter, it is more pleasurable to have friction than not.

It's important to know that many women do not lubricate much during sex. Hormones, stress, and other factors can make a woman dry at times. Please don't use vaginal lubrication as a measure of whether or not a woman is aroused, or worse, whether or not you are a decent lover.

Lubricant can make it easier to enter your partner in certain positions that might otherwise be awkward or if you are using condoms. (Be sure to use a water-based and not oil-based lubricant with a condom, oil just disintegrates rubber.) It is also useful during manual sex, making you able to explore each other for longer periods of time without discomfort.

Here are the five different types of lubricant, their

uses, and reasons to use or not to use them.

Petroleum-based Lubricants

This is the product you find in a jar on the drugstore shelves. It is a very commonly used lubricant, but it isn't especially a nice one. First of all, it has a chemical odor to it that isn't very erotic or romantic. Second, many women find it is irritating to the vulva. It can cause a latex condom to fall apart, and it can stain fabrics.

On the other hand, it will last a long time if you are a man who wants to masturbate, and there will be no embarrassment at the checkout counter.

Please note that many hand and body lotions contain petroleum-based products and so are unsuitable for using with a condom.

Natural Oil Lubricants

These are lubricants that you can find in your cupboard: olive oil, vegetable oil, corn oil, peanut oil, butter and Crisco. Coconut oil also makes a good natural lubricant and smells good, too. The advantage of oils is that they are long lasting, soothing, and great for massage and sexual activities. However, like petroleum-based lubricant, they can stain and also destroy latex condoms.

Water-based Lubricants Containing Glycerin

These are very popular lubricants, making them easy to find. They include Astroglide, KY, Wet, Replens, and Liquibeads. They do work, but some people find that they get sticky due to the glycerin. Also, very important to know, is that glycerin is chemically related to sugar, so if you are prone to yeast infections, use lubricant that does not contain glycerin. They do not, however, stain fabrics and are safe to use with latex condoms.

Water-based Lubricants Not Containing Glycerin

Water-based lubricants like Liquid Silk, Slippery Stuff, Oh My, and Sensual Organics are longer lasting than lubricants

that contain glycerin, do not stain clothing or sheets, and can be used with latex condoms. They are "cushion-y" and so may be preferred for anal experimentation. Some people prefer these lubricants because they feel like a woman's natural lubrication.

Silicone Lubricants

Silicone lubricants have several advantages over their cousins. Silicone lubes include Eros, Venus, Wet Platinum, ID Millennium, and a KY product that is very much like a silicone lubricant called Intrigue They are very long-lasting, slippery, and most people like their feel. They do not have any flavor or odor and can be helpful if you are having sex in a pool or hot tub. They can be used for almost any type of sex play, however.

The drawbacks are that they tend to be expensive (but a little goes a long way) and they cannot be used with silicone or Cyber skin sex toys. Not to be confused with the type of silicone that is used for implants, since massage therapists created silicone lubricant to stay on the skin and not to penetrate it. They are safe to use with condoms.

Toys

Somehow, somewhere, some people got the idea that using a toy for extra pleasure is somehow "cheating." Well, is using a laundry booster "cheating" when you do the laundry? If you add soy sauce to plain rice, is that "cheating"?

There is absolutely nothing wrong with using toys, alone or together. While most men can climax naturally, as they age they may find vibration very pleasant and arousing. And there are many women who take a very long time to climax or can only climax if they have very strong stimulation.

The most popular and basic toy is a vibrator. While you may automatically think of a woman using a vibrator, there is nothing non-masculine about a man using one as well for pleasure and exploration.

There are many different types of vibrators, of

course. Some are long and slender, much like a vibrating dildo, and meant for external and internal stimulation. Others, like the infamous "Rabbit," have extra features that are designed to stimulate the clitoris and / or G-spot. You can also find smooth sculptural vibrators in all kinds of shapes.

So how do you know which kind to choose? Well, one of the reasons there are so many types is that different people like different things. If you can, make a visit to a sex toyshop where models can be demonstrated. Go during the week or early in the day on the weekend so that you don't feel pressured.

If a toyshop is unavailable, or you don't want to visit such a shop, then go online and read descriptions. Some sites also let customers review the products, so you can read those as well.

Once you have purchased a vibrator, plan on using it alone at first. Be sure to examine the vibrator before you use it. Turn the toy on and off, try the different speeds, and make sure it is smooth. Don't just go right for the goods. Use the vibrator on all different parts of your body, both to get used to it and to see what areas feel good.

When you feel ready to go further, use the vibrator on your extremities first, like your hands and feet, and work your way toward your genitals. If you are unfamiliar with the feel of a vibrator on your genitals, go slow and use a light touch at first. Men, especially, might find that a strong vibration will bring them very quickly to orgasm, and going slow can actually prolong the pleasure.

If the vibrator seems too powerful, you can put a towel between you and it. Also, you may find that using a water- or silicon-based lubricant can make exploration more comfortable. And if you are going to insert the toy, it is best to put a condom over it and lubricate the condom.

When you have finished using the vibrator, be sure to wash it very thoroughly in warm water and mild soap, or follow the manufacturer's directions. It is good practice to remove the batteries so that they don't leak and cause problems while the vibrator is stored.

Once you understand how to enjoy the vibrator, introduce it into mutual sex play. There are no rules about how to use toys, so don't make any up except what you need to keep yourself feeling safe and comfortable. Don't forget, too, that there is a whole world of toys to be explored, a tribute to humankind's genius for creating sexual pleasure!

Chapter 14

14. Passion All Your Own

Now that you're on your way to reclaiming your own sexuality, you can start thinking about what YOU want your sex life to be. Being an adult with adult responsibilities is tough. Isn't it great that you can balance it all with a wonderful, intimate, free activity that gives you some of the sweetness you deserve?

Make a commitment to take this sexual journey to passion as true lovers, able to trust one another enough to give and take pleasure as wanted and needed.

Passionate sex really can be experienced as long as you keep an open mind and an open heart. Embracing and understanding your own sexuality, as well as your partner's, can keep this part of your relationship vital as long as you both have the desire and health to maintain it.

If, however, you try on your own to improve your sex life and one or both of you still have difficulty, please know that there is help. There are many great psychotherapists trained specifically in helping people with sexual concerns. You can find a sex therapist certified by the American Association of Sexuality Educators, Counselors, and Therapists by going online to www.aasect.org. If you do not see one listed in your area, do not hesitate to contact the AASECT office for help.

Finally, remember that sex was made pleasurable for a reason—for your enjoyment, and for sharing with a partner. May you both experience the ecstasy that comes with patience, time, and love.

Find out more about Dr. Stephanie Buehler and her products and services:

For sex and relationship information:
www.theblogerotic.com

For sex therapy: *www.thebuehlerinstitute.com*

If you live outside of California and need a sex therapist, please visit the

American Assoc. of Sexuality Educators, Counselors & Therapists at

http://www.aasect.org

Sexual FAQ

While I can't cover all of the problems that a person or couple might have when it comes to sex, I thought I'd give some brief information. Please check www.theblogerotic.com frequently for more detailed sexual problem solving booklets and downloads.

Better yet, sign up on the website for the free e-zine so that you can get great tips for great sex, as well as learn about new products as they are developed.

Q: Why might a man or woman have low sexual desire?

A: There are so many reasons that I cannot list all of them; if this is truly a problem, look for my books on this topic, coming out soon. But here is a basic checklist to give you a start on finding clues. Most of these things sap your energy so that you don't have enough oomph for a lovemaking session:

- Too little sleep

- Poor diet

- Not enough exercise

- Weight gain or weight loss

- Stress

- Worrying

- The blues or outright depression

- Chronic illness and / or medications

- Hormonal problems

- Relationship issues

- Sexual inhibitions

- Poor body image

- Strict upbringing

Try making a real effort to improve your lifestyle. This can often help you manage stress, worry, and mood. You should also get a full check-up from your physician to rule out any underlying medical problems.

Remember, though, that "low desire" sometimes means mismatched desire. If someone wants sex 3-4 times a month, and their partner wants sex every day, that isn't really a case of low desire. Try to understand each other's needs and work out a compromise that will satisfy you both.

Q: Why am I having trouble getting / keeping an erection?

A: There are many physical and psychological

factors that can contribute to erectile dysfunction, or ED. They include:

- Fatigue

- Worry

- Stress

- Depression

- Abuse of alcohol or street drugs

- Cigarettes, both tobacco and marijuana

Finding remedies to reverse the effects of items on this list will often help to resolve the problem.

From a physical standpoint, decreasing levels of testosterone are frequently to blame. As men age, testosterone levels decline about 10% every year, causing them to lose some ability to get or maintain an erection, or to have an erection that is less firm.

The PDE5 inhibitors like Viagra can really help, but so can making sure that you are getting enough stimulation from your partner; taking more time with foreplay; and having intercourse when you are well-rested and relaxed. Even if you don't have an erection, you can still enjoy lovemaking, and you can still bring your partner to orgasm manually, orally, or with a toy.

Q: What can I do about premature ejaculation?

A: There's nothing dangerous about premature ejaculation; it's just annoying to some men and their partners. Premature ejaculation has many different causes, including feeling anxious; being inexperienced as a lover; not making love very often; and a masturbation style that is very quick.

The best way to deal with premature ejaculation is to develop a good awareness of what your body feels like when you think you are going to have an orgasm. Think of the sensations that you have at orgasm as "10" on the scale of letting go, and try to figure out a way to recognize when you are at a 7, 8, and 9 on that scale. When you feel yourself getting to this area on your scale, stop thrusting and take some nice deep breaths until you bring yourself back down to a 5 or 6. It may take some time to learn this technique, but it will be worthwhile.

Q: Why am I having so much trouble having orgasm?

A: There can be many reasons, including unreasonable expectations. Sometimes women just take a long time to "get there." The less frequently you have orgasm, though, the longer it can take. Also, the less you understand your body and what gets you aroused, the more difficult it can be to get the stimulation you need to bring you to orgasm.

The best way to learn how to have orgasm is through masturbation, preferably done alone at first so that you can relax and just learn about your own body. Use some erotic material to get yourself in the mood and take time to touch yourself everywhere, not just your genitals. You can use your fingers or a toy to masturbate.

One of the secrets to orgasm is to touch your self all over the labia and all around the clitoris. Also, some women find that moving as if they are having an orgasm (rocking the pelvis, lifting the buttocks) can help them experience the real thing. Finally, I liken having an orgasm to coaxing a cat down a tree. If you try too hard, it'll never happen! You've got to tease and entice an orgasm to occur. That's the way to have fun instead of making it work.

Also, be sure to read the section on "Toys" in Chapter 12, as a vibrator may be very helpful for you.

Q: What's the best form of birth control?

A: The best form of birth control is one that you'll use! It must also be safe, and it needs to be very effective if you truly don't want to conceive.

Seriously, though, the best form of birth control is abstinence, followed by the oral contraceptive pill (OCP). The worst form of birth control is to do nothing at all; second worst is pulling out before ejaculation; third worst is rhythm method, where you refrain from intercourse when a woman is ovulating.

It stuns me how many smart, educated people have no idea how easy it is to become pregnant. This may be because the media spotlights infertility and difficulties conceiving. The fact is that unprotected intercourse results in pregnancy more frequently than even doctors believed, because research shows that couples tend to have intercourse more often when a woman is fertile. That's because hormonal changes can make a woman want sex more during that time.

Best to talk to your physician about birth control options. Take your partner with you so that you both understand the risks involved. Then pick and stick with it. Don't make excuses. Even though a pregnancy may seem like a "blessed event," planning makes it even more so. Remember: A wanted child is a happier child.

Made in the USA
San Bernardino, CA
13 January 2018